*the*
RELATIONSHIP
*handbook*

## Also by Shakti Gawain

*Awakening*
*Creating True Prosperity*
*Creative Visualization*
*Creative Visualization Deck*
*Creative Visualization Workbook*
*Developing Intuition*
*The Four Levels of Healing*
*Living in the Light*
*Meditations*
*The Path of Transformation*
*Reflections in the Light*

# *the* RELATIONSHIP *handbook*

## *A Path to Consciousness, Healing, and Growth*

# SHAKTI GAWAIN

## *and* GINA VUCCI

Nataraj Publishing

*a division of*

New World Library
Novato, California

Nataraj Publishing
*a division of*

New World Library
14 Pamaron Way
Novato, CA 94949

Text design by Tona Pearce Myers

Library of Congress Cataloging-in-Publication Data
Gawain, Shakti, date.
The relationship handbook : a path to consciousness, healing, and growth / Shakti Gawain and Gina Vucci.
    pages    cm
ISBN 978-1-57731-473-8 (paperback)
    1.  Self-actualization (Psychology) 2.  Interpersonal relations. 3.  Conduct of life.
I. Vucci, Gina. II. Title.
BF637.S4G3935 2014
158.2—dc23                                                              2014031870

First printing, November 2014
ISBN 978-1-60868-473-8
Printed in the USA

 New World Library is proud to be a Gold Certified Environmentally Responsible Publisher. Publisher certification awarded by Green Press Initiative. www.greenpressinitiative.org

10   9   8   7   6   5   4   3   2   1

# Contents

# PART ONE

# INTRODUCTION

# The Path of Relationship

*Most of us have a desire to connect* deeply with others. We long to give and receive love and to share with each other in many ways. Often, however, we find the closeness we desire to be elusive. Relationships of all kinds may come and go, or they may change. At times, relationships can be very painful. Many of us have not had very good role models for relating to others, especially within our families or among those closest to us. We are all doing the best we can to figure out how to be the best parents, friends, partners, brothers, sisters, daughters, and sons to one another. As the old adage goes, "When we were born, they forgot to send the manual!"

Fortunately, we are living in a time of great change and discovery. We're learning new ways of living more consciously, and one of the main ways we are learning is through our relationships. More and more people are seeking help and understanding about how relationships work — not just our intimate partnerships but all our relationships. Many people who seek help for their relationships want to *improve* them (although we tend to secretly think it's the person we're having trouble with who needs to do most of the improving!). A desire to relate to others in a healthier and more fulfilling way is a worthy goal, and learning to communicate effectively can improve all our relationships. Communication is a tool we are continually developing, especially as we grow and change and learn more about ourselves.

Countless psychologists and teachers, with a variety of perspectives and different types of wisdom, focus on helping people improve their relationships. Many of these teachers are extremely effective and very helpful to their clients, but they usually focus on the relationship itself.

There is a different approach to relationships, however. This perspective is not found in popular relationship models, and yet it is the most powerful path to increased awareness that I have ever experienced. *It is the understanding that our relationships are our teachers* and can guide us through our lives if we know how to use them that way. This approach shifts the focus away from the relationship itself and instead looks at what we are experiencing in the relationship and what that can teach us about ourselves and our inner process.

Regardless of whether we stay in a relationship or move on from it, every relationship is an opportunity for us to learn about ourselves and to grow. Working with my relationships in this way has been the most powerful and comprehensive path to consciousness I have experienced, and I love to pass it on to other people.

When we view relationships as a path of consciousness, we recognize that the most important relationship we have is with ourself.

Ultimately, this is our primary relationship, the one that provides the foundation for the rest of our life. All other relationships are mirrors reflecting back to us what we may or may not know about ourselves. The process of using these reflections to learn about our development and ourselves helps us to become conscious, integrated beings. And each of our relationships, when viewed in this way, can become a powerful journey into healing and wholeness.

In this book, you will discover how you can use your relationships as a path to greater awareness. You will find out exactly how problem areas in your relationships reflect valuable lessons you need to learn so that you can experience more fulfillment and satisfaction in life. If you are conflicted about a particular relationship in your life, you will come to recognize that it, like all relationships, offers an opportunity for you to find healing and growth.

In addition to recognizing how you can use your relationships as a path of consciousness, you will also learn how to use tools that bring clarity and healing to your relationships, including creative visualization, affirmations, and Voice Dialogue and facilitation exercises.

Some issues we will work with include the following:

- Becoming aware of and healing our unconscious patterns
- Understanding how to use the "mirror of relationships"
- Using the trouble spots in relationships to guide us toward healing
- Communicating more successfully
- Balancing closeness and independence
- Experiencing more fulfilling relationships with everyone in our lives

The path of consciousness is never-ending and always an adventure. The universe is constantly revealing more to us as we continue on our journey. This book will serve as a guide that you can refer back to time and again as your path continues to unfold.

I wrote this book with Gina Vucci, my longtime manager, friend, and workshop coleader. The book is based on the format of the Relationship Workshop that we have been leading together for years. I open our workshops with an introduction that includes my story, and then I turn it over to Gina to lead exercises exploring creative visualization (which begin and close our workshops) and the transformative work with the selves. The Relationship Workshop is typically held over a weekend, and it has been one of the most powerful workshops we've offered. I am thrilled to be able to share this important work with you through this book.

# Shakti's Story

*I have been fascinated with relationship*, family, and community all my life. As I look back, I can see that at certain times I have deeply longed for closeness and connection. I believe that much of this yearning came from experiences in my early childhood and family.

One reason for this is almost certainly the fact that I was my parents' only child, and they divorced when I was three years old. After they divorced, I lived with my mother. She did not remarry or have other children, so our family was small, just my mother and me. My father remarried, and I gained a lovely stepmother, two stepbrothers, and eventually a half-sister. They lived a few hours' drive away, and I enjoyed visiting them; however, I never lived with them. Though they loved me and I loved them, I felt connected to them in a different way, mainly because I rarely saw them.

My mother's family lived in Texas, and after moving a few times, my mom and I settled in California. We often visited her family for Christmas or Thanksgiving, and I vividly remember how happy I felt being part of a large family for a little while. I think there was a part of me that always wanted more of that feeling.

In my young-adult years, I became enchanted with the fields of psychology, spirituality, and metaphysics. This was in the sixties and seventies, when many Eastern philosophical and spiritual teachings were coming to the West, and many Westerners were traveling to the East.

Like many people in my generation, I spent time traveling in Europe and Asia and was deeply influenced by the different cultures I experienced — especially India. As a typical modern Westerner, I was primarily focused on the mental and physical aspects of life. I was accustomed to approaching my life from a logical viewpoint, and I was driven toward "doing" and achieving. The cultures I was traveling through were oriented toward a more spiritual approach to life, and they cultivated "being" energy. At first, the difference was quite striking to me. Gradually, I began to understand that I needed more balance between doing and being in my life.

By the time I returned to the United States, I knew that I was on a path of personal development, learning to live a more fulfilling life and making a meaningful contribution to the world. I read many books, attended numerous workshops and groups, and went to individual and group therapy. I went to live in a community of fellow seekers that felt like the big family I had always wanted. We meditated together, worked together, and shared with one another the many things we were discovering. We began to give workshops to the public, teaching the things we were learning.

I was making some fascinating discoveries — ideas and tools that were helping me to live a fuller, richer life. Some of these came to me in the form of books, some in the form of workshops, and others in the form of individual teachers. One of my early influences was a book called *The Nature of Personal Reality* by Jane Roberts. It shows how we shape our own experience of reality and proposes that we have the power to create our reality more consciously. This was a radical concept and one I wanted to pursue. I sought additional books on this topic while developing my own ideas about how to apply this process in my life.

Through this work and several serendipitous experiences, I discovered creative visualization, a simple but powerful technique that can help us to create our lives more consciously. We can bring healing into our lives and manifest our wildest dreams through creative visualization exercises, meditations, and affirmations. I also used these practices to raise the level of consciousness in my intimate relationships.

These explorations of my psyche inspired me to lead my own workshops and to work with people individually. I discovered I had a talent for sharing with others the things I had been using in my process. After a while, I got the idea to write a pamphlet containing these ideas that could be helpful to the people in my workshops. This led to self-publishing my books *Creative Visualization* and later *Living in the Light*. Gradually, over the next few years, these underground books became international bestsellers. I never set out to be a successful author or teacher; I just wanted to share the ideas and experiences that were exciting to me. Never in my wildest dreams — or my creative visualizing — did I imagine that my writings would proliferate to the extent that they have. As I have continued to learn new tools and techniques, I have integrated them into my body of work. I have also continued to write and have gone on to publish a total of twelve books.

By the time I was in my midthirties, my books were selling well and I was getting to be very well known. I traveled all over the world speaking, teaching, and leading workshops. I loved it. I had great passion for my work and found working with my students and clients very rewarding. Unfortunately, my work also consumed my life. Too much of my awareness was centered on, connected to, or based in my work, and I started to sense a great imbalance in my life.

My personal life had taken a backseat to my professional life. I was having difficulties with my romantic relationships in particular; I found that difficult patterns were increasingly repeating themselves in those relationships. This became a painful process for me, and I was longing to find a true partner. I wasn't finding the intimate connection I was looking for or the partner I thought I was ready for.

Of course, I only *thought* I was ready. I had done a lot of work on myself, which included a lot of emotional processes. I studied with different teachers, read books, participated in workshops, and went to therapy. But old patterns kept coming up, and in a certain way I felt stuck. The tools that had been working so wonderfully in the other areas of my life didn't seem to be working in the relationship arena. It seemed that a whole other level of my process was being revealed; a deeper level of consciousness was trying to emerge.

Finding myself in this challenging place, I began to visualize some new guidance and direction. I was eventually led to a couple who are therapists and teachers, Dr. Hal Stone and his wife, Dr. Sidra Stone. Through their work, they discovered we have many "selves," aspects within us that act as individual selves with their own ideas, opinions, likes, and dislikes. The Stones developed a technique to dialogue with these selves in a way that brings consciousness to this ongoing process inside us. Their body of work is called "the Psychology of Selves and the Aware Ego," and they call the technique for "talking" with the selves Voice Dialogue. They quickly became my teachers and mentors and now are my dear friends.

When I began to do Voice Dialogue work, I became much more conscious of all the things that were going on inside me. I became more aware of what I was feeling, and I discovered all these different parts of myself that I hadn't even known existed.

Concerning the partner issue, I discovered that I was only in touch with the parts of me that wanted a committed relationship, and so I couldn't understand why it wasn't happening. I was certain that I wanted a relationship and believed I was ready for one. I kept wondering why all the men I was attracted to were unavailable or inappropriate — or lived thousands of miles away! I kept thinking something was wrong with *them*. But, as it turns out, there were some parts of me that I was unconscious of that weren't ready for a partner or didn't want one at all.

All of this seems so obvious now. I was traveling the world teaching that one's outside life reflects what is going on inside, and here I was longing for the right relationship and it wasn't happening. Of course this had to do with a process within myself. When we truly want something and it isn't happening, a part of us is blocking it. In my case, some inner conflict was causing a great deal of ambivalence about relationship and commitment.

I knew I was struggling, but I didn't understand what the struggle was. I developed much more consciousness about what was happening through working with my selves. I began to explore and understand the parts of me that did not want a relationship or were fearful of it. For example, I had always been a strong, independent woman. I was close to forty, and a part of me didn't want to give up my independence or have to compromise with someone else. Another aspect of myself that I discovered was my Caretaker self. I feared, unconsciously, that if I were in a close committed relationship, I would just end up taking care of someone else, and I wouldn't know how to get my own needs met. I had been in a number of relationships where I had been in this role, so I had good reason to fear this would happen.

On a deeper level, there was a child in me who feared opening up and getting close to someone. This aspect, or self, was afraid of being hurt and abandoned — especially because of the pain I experienced as a child when my parents divorced. Other parts of myself were also involved, but these parts were the most dominant in my process.

Now that I had discovered some of the different voices in me, I could clearly feel the ambivalence of these conflicting selves. One of the wonderful things about the Psychology of Selves is that it allows us to be with our ambivalence, acknowledge it, and really hold it. Most of the time, most of us are trying to choose one side or another. We think one part of us is right or that there is a right way to be. We decide we want to be one way or another — "I want to be like this, and I don't want to be like that." Or, "I want this part of me, and I don't want that part of me." This black-or-white way of thinking doesn't work because all parts of us exist, and we can't just wish them away. You can bury and repress them, but sooner or later they come forth, often during a relationship upset or a health crisis. We need *all* of these parts in order to experience true balance in our lives. We need all these selves, although we may not know it.

Voice Dialogue work is about developing consciousness and creating awareness of all of the different selves within us. It's about bringing them all forth and getting in touch with them. When we are aware of the different forces operating within us, we can work with them in different ways. I worked on acknowledging and experiencing — we often call it "holding" — my own ambivalence about relationship, reaching into each part of myself and feeling the parts of me that really wanted partnership *and* feeling the parts of me that really didn't want it. I didn't need to fix this ambivalence or change it; I just needed to be deeply present with it.

In some ways, this point in my story was only the beginning. I have continued to study, learn, and grow through working with my relationships in this way. For now, I will pause my story here, but I have more stories to share with you throughout the book! As we move through the following chapters, we will explore how our various selves are formed, reinforced, or denied.

# PART TWO

# THE POWER *of the* SELVES WITHIN

# Formation of Personality

We *develop our personalities* in ways that are both universal and yet completely unique. We all experience the same process of development, while our individual circumstances and surroundings shape our particular makeup.

When we are born, we are vulnerable, impressionable, and completely reliant on those around us. We develop ways to have our needs met when we are hungry, for example, or uncomfortable, or just need love. Our experiences inform our behaviors; we discover a smile might bring joy and playful interaction or crying might bring comfort and immediate attention.

In that way, our parents, siblings, and those who care for us shape us. Our personalities continue to develop as we explore the best ways to have our needs met. We learn which behaviors will bring us love and acknowledgment and which will bring us negativity and even punishment. These aspects of our personalities evolve and take form as we grow. By adulthood, we have identified the ways that work best for us to operate in the world. As adults, we use similar approaches to our relationships, family, and work life to those we developed in childhood. We have fine-tuned ways of keeping ourselves safe and creating a sense of security in our lives.

A drawback to developing in this way is that we tend to overvalue certain aspects of ourselves. We might even come to think that our way of being in the world is the *only* way to be in the world. And when we overidentify with one aspect or side of ourselves, we automatically create an opposing side, what is often referred to as our *shadow side*.

We value one set of behaviors or certain parts of ourselves and then consider the other parts unacceptable, "not good," or even a liability. We see our way as good and right, and we actually try to disown the other parts of us or deny they exist. Additionally, we form rules about how we should be, and how others should be, based on this value system. As a result, we criticize ourselves when we express or show our shadow parts, and we judge other people when they display these behaviors.

Most likely we have revealed some of these shadow aspects of ourselves at some point in our lives. If we received a negative reaction when we exhibited a certain part of ourselves, though, we probably learned to hide or suppress it. Eventually, we learned that showing that part of ourselves was not safe and would not get our needs met. For example, one aspect we often choose not to express is what we refer to as our "vulnerability." Our vulnerability is the part within us that is connected to our sensitivity, our needs, and our emotions. If we have shown vulnerability in the past, we may have been criticized or ignored. In order to feel safe or in control, we might "stuff" these feelings and needs and act instead like we don't have them.

Consider a sensitive child who is quick to show her feelings, from happiness to sadness, enthusiasm to anxiety. If she is told she is too sensitive, shouldn't take things so seriously, or has no good reason to worry or be sad, she will learn to conceal or deny her emotions. Just seeing that her expressed feelings worry or anger those around her would be enough for her to become adept at suppressing them.

Because she has learned that a more detached approach to life pleases others, she comes to see that this way of relationship is the right and ideal way to be. She comes to view sensitivity and emotionality as a negative thing in herself — and in others. She criticizes herself when she expresses these parts of herself and judges other people who display them. Our unexpressed aspects — whether vulnerability, boldness, creativity, daring, sexuality, or others — don't disappear. They continue to exist "in the shadows," and like most hidden things, they come out one way or another, sooner or later.

What's more, failing to recognize and find room for our shadow sides limits how we experience and participate in our lives. Our relationships will be affected if we think it's wrong or weak to express our feelings. If we value intellect but not creativity or the arts, we may choose a career that becomes increasingly dissatisfying. Our well-being depends on our being whole and having access to all of who we are.

All the parts of ourselves — those that we consciously develop and our shadow sides — are our "selves." We use the term "selves" to describe aspects within our personality; in Jungian psychology, the selves are called "subpersonalities." Each of these selves has its own perspective on our lives, its own ideas, and even its own ways of remembering specific events.

It is important to note here that we are in no way talking about multiple personality disorder. Multiple personality disorder is a psychiatric dissociative disorder. Here, we are bringing to the light a simple process that is naturally occurring within us all the time. It is as simple as sensing two different parts of us when we go out to eat — part of us wants to eat healthy and another part wants to order off the dessert menu. It is the conflict we feel when making choices, ranging from major life changes to simple daily decisions. This work was inspired by and is most similar to Jung's work with the shadow and discovering the unconscious.

As mentioned earlier, I was first introduced to working with these aspects by Drs. Hal and Sidra Stone. The basic idea of their work, which they call the Psychology of Selves, is that we have within us the potential for every energy or aspect of personality that exists, and each of us develops the aspects that work best in our lives to get our needs met, and we minimize or disregard the aspects that do not.

I believe that our work in this lifetime is to create awareness of *all* the parts of ourselves. Each part has a purpose, has information for us, and is actually necessary for us to achieve the balance and wholeness we are searching for. Ultimately, coming to embrace all our selves is the path to enjoying more balance in our relationships as well.

First, let's look at our primary selves.

# Discovering Our Primary Selves

*Our primary selves are the main ways* we interact with the world, and they are how most people experience us or would describe us. We usually love these parts of ourselves and feel quite proud of these aspects. We become closely identified with our primary selves and think they are who we are. Until we become conscious of the Psychology of Selves and learn to give voice to the many other selves within us, our primary selves really run our lives.

Within us, certain selves that work together and have similar qualities, perspectives, and complementary ways of being form groups. They work together for a common purpose: to have us behave in a certain way that will keep us safe and ensure that our needs are met. They also work together to reinforce what they believe is right. They work on our behalf and facilitate our getting through life, developing our careers, finding the right partners, and raising our families.

For example, we might develop a personality, or group of selves, that reflects one of our parents. If this is our mother, we adopt the ways that she interacts in the world and form a belief that her ways are true and correct. We mimic her in many ways, though we put our own spin on it.

Or maybe the opposite happens: we form a group of selves that are in direct contrast to one or both of our parents. We might think that the way our mother raised us was lacking or flawed in some respect, and we decide never to be like her, or at least not to parent the way she did. We might decide that how she lived her life was wrong, and so we behave in an opposite way, hoping to avoid the challenges or consequences she might have experienced. This is especially common when there has been mental illness, abuse, alcoholism, or drug addiction in the family.

Whether we adopt or reject our parents' primary selves, we all develop the best ways to keep ourselves safe and get our basic needs met. As with all children, I took in the values and ways of doing things that were around me when I was growing up. My primary personality was developed out of what I saw and experienced from my environment. I came from an intellectual family, where analytical, rational, pragmatic thinking was highly valued. Because of this, I developed my mental, intellectual capacity; being rational and articulate became a large part of my personality. I received acknowledgment and was rewarded for these pursuits, which further reinforced and strengthened them within me.

Another self that developed in me was the extremely responsible one. This was probably a reaction to my parents getting divorced when I was very young. My mom was single and raised me on her own, and so by being responsible I could make her life easier and help her in any way she needed. Along with being responsible, I became very independent. My mom was burdened with work in addition to the many other things that she needed to do or handle. Through being responsible and independent, I attempted to share her burden and alleviate any additional stress or worry she might experience.

In addition to these more powerful selves, I also had some vulnerable aspects. I became a very sensitive child. I was acutely aware of what my parents or those around me were feeling or experiencing. I developed a strong caretaker quality to help my mother and to support her. I was sensitive to those in pain, and I would intuit what they needed or were feeling. In truth, this way of being was one of the main ways that I got through life: taking care of others, pleasing other people, and making other people happy. I have always focused on the needs of other people in my life.

I developed these behaviors in response to my childhood environment, and I adopted traits that were modeled for me by my mother. She was exceedingly bright and skillful at doing many things. (And still is!) I saw her as strong, competent, and hardworking. It became important to me to be highly competent as well, managing many things and being successful at whatever I decided to do. Being rational, responsible, and independent helped me to do this.

During my formative years, my mom was quite a powerful person in many ways. She was adventurous and bold. She became a city manager at a time when few women held these kinds of jobs. She traveled the world, and she got into yoga and meditation many decades ago.

I admired her, and I too developed these strengths. Ultimately, I became comfortable with a certain amount of power. I also valued taking risks, adventurous travel, and learning about other cultures. In my twenties I went on a journey around the world with a friend, with only a few hundred dollars in my pocket.

These are just a few of my primary selves. They work in partnership with some other selves, like my Perfectionist self, who makes sure I am doing everything to the highest standard; my Inner Critic, who lets me know when I am falling short; and my Pusher self, who keeps me going and crosses everything off my to-do lists.

These selves are common in many of us, and they often have the most power over our personalities and the way we relate to others and in our day-to-day life. They manifest themselves or operate differently in different people, but they essentially function in similar roles.

My primary selves have been developed substantially over time and are the parts I have identified with for a very long time. They represent who I've been — and to their credit, they have gotten me a long way in life. They've helped me to become successful, to write books, to teach, and to make a difference in people's lives. These primary selves have been good for me in many ways and have served me well.

## EXERCISE
### *Identifying Your Primary Selves*

This simple, powerful exercise can help you identify your primary selves. It only takes a few minutes.

Take a moment to close your eyes and think about yourself. What kind of person are you? What are some of your main personality traits? If someone just met you, how might they describe you?

Now take a piece of paper and at the top write, "I am…" Then, down the left-hand side, make a list of ten to twelve single-word descriptions that quickly and easily come to mind. List the aspects, characteristics, and traits that describe you in a general way. Think of someone who knows you as an acquaintance; how might they describe you? (This list may not reflect the ways that people who know you well might describe you. In intimate relationships with close friends or family, we tend to reveal more of ourselves and behave in different ways.) It is best to jot down what comes to you without thinking about it too much. If you come up with fewer than twelve words, that's fine.

Here is an example of how Gina, my workshop coleader, completed the exercise. First, she wrote a snapshot of her life. It might help you to also jot down a similar snapshot of your life.

> I am a single mother with three children. I work full time and volunteer regularly. I am active with family commitments and community events.

I am…

> Strong
> Independent
> Outgoing
> Mothering
> Responsible
> Loving

Smart
Forthright
Caring
Generous

Review your list. What do you think? What observations do you have about the list? Is there anything new to you or surprising? This list is most likely a list of your primary selves, especially if you feel proud as you review the list!

Although your list might be full of positive attributes, it is common to have negative descriptions as well. Not all of our primary selves are positive! Once we discover our primary selves, the next step is to take a clear look at our other selves — those we have ignored, forgotten, or even hidden somewhere deep within: our shadow selves.

# Learning from Our Shadow Sides

*As we have seen,* our primary selves are strong energies that get us through life. They are shaped by our upbringing and evolve over time as they are further influenced by our life experiences. Our primary selves guide us and direct us, and they are the driving force in the creation of our lives. They do so even if we have not recognized them.

Our primary selves may dominate our thoughts and actions a majority of the time, 90 percent or more. However, our primary selves are still only *part* of who we are. Although these selves succeeded in ensuring that our early needs were met, and they feel very comfortable and familiar to us, they may not have the best answers for how to live our lives today.

Just as we develop and feel comfortable with certain aspects of ourselves, we disown and deny other parts we are not comfortable with. We find ourselves lopsided in a sense, having full access to certain ways of being in the world and little or no access to other ways of being. This limits, and can even prevent, our ability to find fulfillment, wholeness, and balance in our lives.

Over time, we might begin to feel stuck or feel that something is missing. We might describe our life or ourselves as feeling out of balance. We may develop a desire to reject aspects of our lives, routines, or commitments. We may also experience a strong urge to create something opposite and radically different from the life we've been living. Sometimes this is called a "midlife crisis," though it can happen at any age and at any time.

If we are married or in a committed partnership (though this can happen in any relationship), we might feel stymied, trapped, bored, or more like a sibling to our partner than a lover. In other relationships we may feel distant and alienated, rebellious, or relentlessly argumentative. We may find ourselves in regular conflict with specific types of people, or we may covet what others have or envy how they live their lives.

When we begin the process of exploring the various selves within us, we discover that we are disproportionately identified with certain aspects of ourselves, which means that we ultimately deny and disown other parts, as mentioned above. Our rejection of certain people in our lives is actually an attempt to distance ourselves from the parts we're rejecting within ourselves. In reality, it is not other people or events that elicit our reactions. The qualities we are rejecting within ourselves are merely being reflected in the situations and relationships in which we are experiencing difficulty.

This is the next central aspect in the Psychology of Selves: discovering our *disowned selves* and learning from our shadow sides.

These are the parts within us that we have disconnected from, rejected, denied. They do exist, however, and they actually hold the key to finding the balance and wholeness we are seeking in our lives. In fact, they are the exact ingredients we are looking for as we struggle to get out of this "stuck" feeling and the imbalance we are experiencing. The clue we are missing, the specific "medicine" to cure our unique malady, is already within us. Our work is to uncover and integrate these parts of us. This begins an exciting and rewarding lifelong journey of discovery.

I remember vividly when I began to feel out of balance. I felt restless and somewhat uncomfortable. Certain areas of my life felt developed, successful, and abundant, while other areas of my life felt messy, and I was baffled as to why they were not working out. After learning about my different selves, I came to understand that my primary selves had taken over my life to such an extent that other parts of me had no room whatsoever. I needed to become aware of these selves and learn to acknowledge and accept them. Given what I've said about my primary selves, can you guess what some of my disowned selves were?

Being carefree, playful, and spontaneous were aspects of a child-like self that was definitely disowned in me. These energies are the opposites of many of my primary selves, especially my intellectual, rational, and pragmatic selves. I was so thoroughly identified with all aspects of "doing," or "knowing," that I had no primary selves that were related to mindless activities, including relaxing or resting.

I also felt very serious about "saving the world." My sense of responsibility and caretaking extended to wanting to work toward this goal (like many of my generation). This meant that activities

I deemed frivolous had little room in my life. How could I play or enjoy myself when the environment was in peril, the government a mess, and so many in the world suffering? One result of this way of thinking was that my creativity was disowned. If a pursuit had concrete value or purpose, I would do it. If it didn't, then I wouldn't participate. Today, I am deeply involved in singing and music, and I enjoy brushing up on my Italian. These activities might not "save the world," but as they renew me, I think they also invigorate my efforts in the world at large. These hobbies are exactly what I needed to bring a deeper experience of richness into my life.

Many selves related to receiving were also disowned within me. Given my responsible and independent selves, I handled many things at once and got everything done. It was hard for me to ask for help or to allow others to do something for me. Also, I was so identified with my caretaking role that I was completely disconnected from having my own needs met. I focused the majority of my attention on others and what they needed, often leaving myself feeling uncared for. Now I am better able to balance this in my life and have learned much more about how to take care of myself.

The following exercise will help you to uncover your most prominent disowned selves.

## EXERCISE

### *Identifying Your Disowned Selves*

Go back to the list you made in the "Identifying Your Primary Selves" exercise (pages 24–26), and start a second column down the right-hand side of the page under the title "Opposite..." Write a one-word description that is the opposite of the trait you wrote on the left. Do this somewhat quickly, without a lot of thought. Just read the word on the left and write what comes to mind on the right. Try not to overthink it.

As an example, here is Gina's original list along with her list of opposites:

| I am... | Opposite... |
|---|---|
| Strong | Weak |
| Independent | Needy |
| Outgoing | Withdrawn |
| Mothering | Needy/Childlike |
| Responsible | Irresponsible |
| Loving | Mean |
| Smart | Stupid |
| Forthright | Deceitful or dishonest |
| Caring | Cold |
| Generous | Stingy |

Once you complete the right-hand column, take a moment to review your list. What observations do you have about the traits you just wrote down? What conclusions might you draw about yourself from this list? Do you notice any judgmental or critical terms in the right column? Is there a term that is repeated more than once?

This list offers us insight into what might be disowned within us. It represents what we might be denying in our lives, our shadow sides. It's common to recognize qualities in the right-hand column that you dislike in other people. You might even notice that your list describes someone in particular in your life; if so, this person may be reflecting a shadow side. For example, perhaps you have a friend whose "neediness" rubs you the wrong way, or a coworker on your team who is "irresponsible," or you are trying to salvage a relationship with a partner who is "uncommunicative."

If you have thought of a person who embodies one or more of your right-column descriptions, reflect on that person. It could be someone you hold quite dear despite this trait. Or it could be someone you feel great aversion toward. Think about the thing you dislike. What buttons does your partner's irresponsibility or your dear friend's neediness push in you? Why do you think that is? How did you come to be put off by irresponsibility and neediness and, conversely, to value responsibility and self-sufficiency?

The more critical or judgmental the term in the right-hand column is, the greater the degree to which that aspect is disowned within you. So the person you are judging is reflecting something you are missing or minimizing in your life.

It may be difficult to do so, but take a moment to consider what it would be like to have those "negative" traits yourself. How might your life be different? How would it feel? Is there any sense of freedom or relief at the thought of sometimes being needy or irresponsible?

## CHOICES: IDENTIFYING THE POSITIVE ASPECTS OF DISOWNED SELVES

When reviewing the characteristics in your "opposite" list, you may not see any reason to want to have those qualities. You may be asking, "Why would I ever want to be irresponsible or needy?" In this work, it is critical we focus on the essence or essential quality of the characteristic, not on the actual behavior of the other person. If we focus on the other person's expression of that trait, we miss the opportunity to learn from the experience. The truth is that we need access to all parts of ourselves to experience authentic wholeness and balance. The ways we bring these parts of ourselves into our lives will look different (especially from the person we are judging), but we need to be able to draw on all of the energies available to us and, in doing so, find the balance that is right for us.

For example, you might not want "irresponsible" on your tombstone, but perhaps you don't always have to be the most responsible person in the room, in a relationship, in your department, and so on. Neediness might disturb you because it makes you feel weak or childlike, but aren't there times when you do need to lean on the strength of others or to experience sympathy and comforting? Take some time with your right-hand column with these things in mind. Watch for what is revealed.

I like to use this lighthearted example as another way to describe the experience of stepping back from our primary selves and recognizing our disowned selves: It is as if our head is stuck in a bowl of fruit. All we can see is an orange and a banana right in front of our eyes. That's all we can see, all we know, and the only options to choose from. When we pull back, and pull our faces out of the bowl, we see there are many fruits in the bowl, including grapes, apples, kiwis, and mangoes! We find there are many varieties and we have many choices. Similarly, when we take a step back in our lives, we can see that there are other parts of ourselves that we didn't see before; there are many different ways of thinking and acting that we didn't know about. We find that they all contribute to a rich, colorful, and sweet life experience.

Let's go back to our lists for a moment. Here are Gina's reflections and insights on her different selves:

> On the left side of my list, I described myself as "strong" and then wrote "weak" as the opposite on the right side. Once I came to understand that the opposite aspect I had identified — or its underlying energy — was my key to freedom, I had to ask myself, "What value could I possibly find in being weak?" To me, there was nothing good that could possibly come from being weak. When you're weak, people step on you, take advantage of you, maybe even abuse you.
>
> After working with this process, I found that by always being strong, I never allowed myself to have feelings. I always had to be strong for those around me, and I was unable to experience any down side in life or grieve losses from my childhood. I realized I had been this way since I was a young girl, including never grieving the loss of my father when I was nine because I believed I had to be strong for the rest of my family. On a basic level, I also never allowed myself to rest or even take a day off. I shouldered every family tragedy with perseverance and optimism, even if that's not how I was feeling. This way of being became extremely overwhelming. By "owning" more of the "weak" energy, I could allow others to care for me when I needed it. When I stopped disowning my very real "weakness," I could ask for help, ask for directions, even lean on others for support. I could rest when I needed to, even indulge in reading a book for a couple hours! I found that I didn't have to fight every adversity that came along. I came to realize that there was no rulebook on how to get

through life's difficulties gracefully. There wasn't some handout I had missed, and so I could make mistakes, too. I was able to finally retire the superhero cape.

Another set of opposite selves I had on my list was "independent" and "needy." In addition, I also had "needy/childlike" as an opposite to another primary self, "mother." Having the same trait listed more than once often points to a deeply disowned self. What made this such a sensitive issue for me?

When I thought about being independent or being a mother, I felt a lot of gratification, honor, and pride. I felt powerful, even impervious on some level. I imagined myself like one of those women carved into the front of Viking ships, mighty and fearless, leading her crew through the turbulent and stormy seas.

Once I began this work, however, I was able to see that I had actually been feeling stuck for quite a while. I realized that I thought I had to have answers for every situation that arose. I thought that I needed to respond to and care for everyone who needed it. Often I concluded that others were just not able to take care of themselves properly, and I found their neediness embarrassing. This way of living became exhausting. Once I was able to access some of the energy of being "needy," I could recognize that I didn't have to do everything myself.

Ultimately, I was able to see that what I had viewed as being needy wasn't really neediness at all. It was simply the desire to have my basic needs met — to care for myself, to value myself, and to love myself, I learned to ask for help when I needed it. I was able to take time for myself and spend it on activities that I enjoyed and found rewarding. I could now see that this wasn't a liability or something to eradicate in myself — in fact, it meant freedom for me.

Another opposite was "irresponsible." Who would want to be irresponsible? I reflected on my life and realized that for every party I brought food, *and* drinks, *and* dessert. For every sports team my children were on, I was a team parent or coach, and I volunteered for several other commitments as well. I began to see the imbalance in this way of being and how exhausting and stressful it was. I realized that if I took on fewer commitments, I would have more time for myself and more time to spend with my family, too.

I came to the conclusion that I was not being irresponsible or passive by not taking on more responsibilities. I found I could participate without running the show, and when I stepped back, I made room for others to participate and become involved. It was not my job to make it all work out! Now I can make conscious choices about what I take on and not feel like I have to do something I would rather not do.

The disowned selves within us hold the key to creating balance and finding fulfillment in our lives. They may not seem as if they hold any value, but we find that they hold the perfect essence or quality we are missing to create wholeness in our lives. We have been walking through life with a limited set of lenses and often have a very narrow view of life. Through opening to our disowned selves, we see so many different aspects to a situation. We see different qualities in other people and in ourselves. We recognize possibilities we could not see before and find solutions we would have never considered.

There are a large number of possibilities of primary and disowned selves. Whatever you experience is true for you. Gina and I have shared just a few examples from our experiences; however, each person can have entirely different experiences with different selves. In the chapter "Exploring Common Selves" we share detailed descriptions of primary selves to help you further identify some of your selves.

Next, in part 3, we will see what amazing insights can be learned from our relationships, regardless of whether or not the relationship itself felt like a positive one.

# PART THREE

# RELATIONSHIP
## *as* TEACHER

# Relationships as Mirrors

*Identifying our disowned selves* is one of the ways we can use our relationships as reflections, and by going through this process, we have the opportunity to see in ourselves what we might not have been able to see otherwise.

Once we learn how to use these reflections, our relationships can become one of the most powerful avenues we have for becoming conscious. We see what a great value all of our relationships are and what amazing gifts they hold for us. Any and every relationship in our lives — with our friends, coworkers, neighbors, children, and other family members as well as our primary partners — can be a reflection to us in this way. Even an encounter with a stranger can sometimes be an important learning experience. It's very difficult to look inside ourselves and see what's going on in there, particularly to see what we're unaware of. That's why it's important to look at our relationships as mirrors of our inner processes. Used in this way, relationships become one of the most valuable sources of healing and teaching in our lives.

Different relationships offer different opportunities to practice this work. I have found the following exercises very helpful — one helps us focus on positive reflections with people we admire, and the other looks at our judgments and negative reflections.

## Positive Reflections

Some of our relationships reflect to us in a "positive" way, meaning they mirror parts of ourselves that are familiar and that we feel comfortable with. Think of someone you admire. Think about how they inspire you, and maybe how you wish you were like them in a certain way or how you feel when you are with them. What do they do that you admire? What are the exact qualities that you are attracted to? Take a moment to think about these and then jot them down. Try to use one or two words or short phrases to describe these qualities.

Review your list of admirable qualities — what do you see about yourself? Do you see ways you might be similar to the person you admire? Or, are these qualities you wish you had or you think you should have?

This exercise generally reveals many positive reflections. When we identify what we admire in other people, these are often aspects that we like and want more of in our lives. In fact, when we recognize a quality in someone else, it is most often because we have it, too. One of our favorite phrases is, "You spot it, you've got it!" When we see a positive quality in someone else, we most likely possess it as well, but maybe we have difficulty accessing it or truly owning it in our lives. Once we identify it and get in touch with it, we can practice bringing it into our lives with intention. We can also use meditation time to practice accessing it, visualizing ourselves fully embracing and expressing this aspect of ourselves.

On the other hand, we may not recognize one or more of the characteristics from this list within ourselves. We might see ourselves as lacking this quality or even being completely different from this person. This is not a negative criticism; we just recognize we don't see in ourselves a quality we admire. If we look at the quality we have identified in the other person, however, and focus on the underlying essence of that quality, we most likely can see how we, in fact, do carry that energy. Although we may express it differently, in our own unique way, we usually carry it somewhere within us and have access to it.

We can also gain insight in situations where we admire a quality or person too much. When we do this, we are usually comparing ourselves to the person and seeing how we fall short. This way of thinking generally reveals our self-criticism. Recognizing this may shed light on a limiting belief we have created and continue to hold: that we can't have that quality or be that way.

As an example, let's look at two friends. Isla admires her friend Kelley. She sees her as outgoing, funny, smart, and well-liked. "She gets along with everybody!" Isla says. In this simple exercise, Isla identifies the qualities she looks for in a friendship.

But although Isla admires Kelley, she also compares herself to Kelley in a way that makes herself feel inadequate. Isla feels that people don't like her in the way they like Kelley. She thinks she doesn't get along with people as well as Kelley does. In this way, admiring Kelley has become a way for Isla to criticize what's "wrong" with herself.

Interestingly, by examining "positive reflections" in relationships, we can bring to light negative thought patterns or a negative dialogue we are having internally. We might be talking to ourselves in a critical way and not even be conscious of it. We are holding ourselves back and don't even know it.

Through this exercise, Isla came to see that she doubted herself. She learned to see this as the voice of her Inner Critic. She became more aware of what this critic was telling her, and she could see how this kind of criticism was undermining her.

Isla began working with her critical voice and listening to what it had to say. As she understood where her critic was coming from and what it was concerned with, this self became more supportive. The fear of the critic was that if Isla put herself out there, she would be rejected. This had happened to her before, and it was a painful dynamic from her childhood. Isla saw that her critical voice was in fact trying to protect her. Yet she also saw how she could be more confident and put less importance on her Inner Critic's fears about what others thought. She could take care of herself in new ways and trust that it was safe for her to be more outgoing socially; she could bring more of the qualities she admires in Kelley to the surface in herself. This was exciting and freeing for her.

## NEGATIVE REFLECTIONS: JUDGMENTS

When we can look honestly at our ourselves and our relationships, we become open to the lessons and insights that they offer to us. Relationships reveal to us where we might have work to do. The people we are in relationship with, even when the interactions are brief, reflect back to us our beliefs, opinions, judgments, likes, and dislikes. At the same time, we are reflecting to others the ideas, beliefs, and preferences they hold about themselves.

For our next exercise, think of someone you dislike. This can be an actual person, a type of person, a group of people, or a list of qualities that really irritate you.

For this exercise during one of our workshops, a majority of participants coincidentally chose a particular politician as their example. They got really fired up, describing him as selfish, reckless, careless, stupid, a liar, power hungry, and unconcerned about people who were suffering or in need. Although we primarily use this exercise with people we are in relationship with, it can also be helpful to use public figures. The distance in these relationships can allow us to see more objectively and with more humor.

The value our judgments hold is that they reflect to us where we may be out of balance or in denial about our *own* behaviors. They point us to what is often disowned within us — our shadow side. These qualities often hold potentially vital energies we really need but may be rejecting. We have found a way to reap the benefits of our judgments, and it involves looking at the essential energy or quality that underlies the objectionable characteristic we have identified.

In working with our rowdy group of workshop attendees, we broke down the different characteristics they named and felt very angry about. We started with "selfish." Now, who would want to be selfish? What good could there possibly be in being selfish? We asked the group to consider the underlying essence of being selfish and to ask: What does being selfish really mean?

Being selfish can represent a variety of behaviors. We identified the essence of "being selfish" as putting our focus on ourselves. This could simply be a matter of setting boundaries in our lives. It could also be self-care or taking care of ourselves so we might care for others in some way. Through this exercise, many people in the workshop realized that, once they took the focus off the politician and looked at this aspect in their personal lives, many of them were overly focused on others. They saw how they put everyone else's needs before their own. They saw how they carried guilt whenever they thought of themselves before someone else, especially people in their family. From this perspective, it was obvious how being selfish was disowned for many of them. It represented a positive quality that most of them actually needed more of in their lives.

Viewed in this way, they could see that having some "selfishness" was a good thing. Being able to say "no" when they needed to was actually important. They needed this quality in their lives to restore balance and healing, both mentally and physically. Identifying a negative reflection revealed an important and necessary part of their lives that was missing for many of them. By realizing this, they were able to consciously own more of that energy. Honestly looking at and embracing their need to take care of themselves brought about a sense of well-being and ease.

Another aspect on the list we examined was being "stupid." We asked ourselves: What could possibly be the essential quality underlying "stupid"? Who, after all, wants to be stupid? One participant in particular, Donald, spoke up about how this characteristic applied in his own life. Although he despised the politician and ridiculed him for all the gaffes and ignorant statements he made, Donald saw how being "stupid" in his own life meant not always having answers and not knowing everything. He realized his role in his family was to be the go-to person for everyone else. This was also his role at work, where he constantly solved other people's problems. By owning being "stupid," Donald could relieve the pressure he put on himself of always being the one with the answers. It meant that he didn't have to take care of everyone else, and he could relax a bit.

Donald had grown up with an alcoholic father, and he looked down on him and thought he was a "stupid" drunk. He had internalized needing to be "smart" so that he would never follow in the path of his father. He eventually saw that his father was actually a very loving man who had a disease, and in fact his father had sobered up and had remained sober for many years. Through this exercise, Donald became much more aware of all the pressure he unconsciously put on himself, and he felt a powerful new sense of forgiveness for both his father and himself.

Donald also realized that the intimacy he had been longing for in his relationship with his wife was affected by his inability to be authentic, which for him meant not always knowing how to fix something or how to solve a problem. He had never been able to ask her for help or be vulnerable with her in any way. By getting in touch with this part of himself — the vulnerable part, the part that doesn't know things, the "stupid" part — he felt he could experience more of a partnership with his wife. Donald realized that he could be vulnerable with her, and that this would actually bring them closer.

In their judgment of the politician, our group discussed the phrase "power hungry." Sheri thought "power hungry" was particularly offensive, the worst thing on the list. Although being power hungry is similar to being selfish, she thought it was worse because it also represented aggressive and macho behaviors, which were totally unacceptable qualities to her.

Then Sheri examined "power hungry" as it reflected on herself and her own process, and she had a major "ah-ha" moment. When we asked ourselves what value there was in being "power hungry," Sheri said it could be about owning power, not power over others, but her own personal power within.

Sheri described issues she'd had with a series of bosses. Each boss had been focused on their own next promotion and had used her to help them get what they wanted. Each time, she felt thrust into a thankless and dismissive role, and she realized that she had been afraid to own her power. What would happen if she stood up for herself? What would happen if she put forth what she wanted? What if she wanted to move up in the company? These questions helped her to realize how she had been making herself small and subservient to others.

Sheri was so afraid of being criticized and of failure that she kept herself stuck in minor jobs. The cycle repeated itself over and over as it played out with each new boss. She realized she did have aspirations and wanted more responsibilities, but she had been stifling that voice within herself because of her fears. As she experienced these realizations, Sheri felt a completely new sense of power within herself. She did not feel above her colleagues or bosses, but equal to them. She saw the value of her contributions, suggestions, and talents, and she saw the value she could bring to her company by sharing her newfound "power."

## When Relationships Mirror Opposite Qualities

When we examine negative reflections in our relationships with others, we start by looking at qualities we are highly judgmental of, and then we search for the value that the essence of these qualities can bring into our lives. Another signal that we are identifying a dismissed self or quality is when we find ourselves in a relationship with someone who exemplifies our "opposite."

For example, let's look at two coworkers. Alice is an account manager. She is very organized, structured, and detail-oriented. Dorothy is a creative manager. She is an expansive thinker, connects with clients well, and is a great visionary. They clash whenever an incomplete project nears its deadline. Alice feels frustrated with Dorothy's "dreaminess," especially when she is still coming up with new ideas rather than finishing the project, and Dorothy feels stifled by Alice's micromanagement and inflexibility.

As we examine what might be happening using our relationship model, we can see that they are each "carrying" or acting out opposite behaviors. They are reflecting opposite traits toward each other. Each is also "overidentifying" with aspects of their own personalities. To make matters worse, they both feel they're right!

In any relationship, if we can take the emphasis off of the actual behaviors and look deeper, at the essential qualities underlying our and our partner's actions, we can view the dynamic with more objectivity. We can recognize any aspects of our personalities that we may be overidentifying with and any aspects we may be rejecting or denying. To experience wholeness and balance in our lives, we need to be able to access all the possible energies available, or at least become aware of the essence of each of these characteristics.

Using this relationship model, Dorothy and Alice discovered what was happening in their dynamic and used this as a team-building exercise at their workplace. They were each able to see that they had blinders on when it came to their own behavior and that they were not valuing each other's contributions. Alice was able to recognize Dorothy's work style, and instead of trying to get her to work differently, she reworked her timeline to allow the creative process to unfold and ultimately produce a richer product in the end. Alice was able to balance her need for a timeline with Dorothy's need for creative space.

Alice also recognized that she felt particularly triggered by her fears of a client's criticism. She is hypersensitive to criticism and has always felt anxious about pleasing the client. Without realizing it, Alice was trying to control Dorothy in an attempt to control the feelings she was having.

Through this process, Dorothy also came to value Alice's role as the project manager. By having a partner who could manage the clients and logistics, Dorothy had space to explore her creativity and to create what the client was looking for. Dorothy also saw the benefit of containing her process so that she could successfully meet her clients' deadlines. Further, she realized that deadlines were feeling constricting because of issues in her own creative process. Dorothy's Inner Critic was very strong, and she was taking longer on projects than necessary because she was second-guessing herself the entire time, which caused her to repeat steps several times.

Using relationships as mirrors is a type of inner work that can help in any scenario. There are as many variations or possibilities as there are individuals. You can see by the few examples here how rich they are with discovery and insight.

While these exercises are helpful and easy to apply in any situation, they are especially helpful when you have a conflict with someone, such as in an argument when you find yourself saying, "You are so _____ [fill in the blank]!" This is a perfect time to use your feelings to examine what is going on inside you. We can't change the other person or get them to stop what they are doing that is so upsetting to us, but we can use our reactions to redirect ourselves. What we can do is work within ourselves and within our own lives. It is amazing how people become less annoying once we begin to look at ourselves and gain insight into what is going on with us!

Our relationships with other people continually reflect exactly where we are in our process of becoming whole. Each day is an opportunity for us to practice. If we take the approach that our life is one big human experiment, then every experience we have is just a part of that process. We can approach each day, each moment, with openness and with the awareness that every person we meet, every situation we find ourselves in, and every interaction we have is an opportunity for us to learn more about ourselves. We cannot seize all of these opportunities, but we try to catch as many as we can! With this attitude, we can take more experiences in stride and turn them into experiences that help us grow.

We have now explored a variety of ways of viewing relationships as teachers and guides. This process is not always simple or painless, but we can grow as individuals and create more gratifying relationships in these ways. Now we will look at how all our selves come together to create the person we are and explore some of the common selves we all seem to share.

# The Aware Ego and the Inner Child

*We are each born with great potential;* every one of us can access all the energies of all selves that exist in the world, for they are all aspects of ourselves. These aspects are deeply affected by those who raise us and influenced by our environment, and so there are a large number of possibilities for the different selves, or groups of selves, that can form within us. These groups of selves continue to be shaped through our life experiences, which alters their depth and complexity even further.

Within these variations and possibilities, I have found that in general there is a group of selves that form our archetypes — a core group of selves that have certain patterns and play certain roles in our lives. All of us have these selves within us and experience them to some degree and in some form. In the next chapter, "Exploring Common Selves," we will look at some of these selves in detail.

But first, let's discuss awareness and the ego itself. As we use relationships as teachers, we begin to recognize the different selves within us. We come to understand those aspects we have strongly developed and those others we have denied. Through this process, we begin to experience "awareness," or an experience of being fully present in the moment. Awareness is simply witnessing or observing what is. Awareness has no investment or influence in the process, nor is it a proactive experience. As many know who have sought to experience awareness and a sense of being in the present moment, this is often a short-lived, even fleeting experience.

In identifying and talking with the selves, we experience awareness when we recognize a self as *part* of who we are and not *all* of who we are. Awareness also arises when we recognize that, for every acknowledged self, there is an equal and opposite energy or self that we have not acknowledged, accepted, or integrated into our way of being. This experience of awareness leads to the process of becoming conscious.

Awareness is a delightful place to exist in; it's expansive, peaceful, even blissful. However, this is not a position from which we can take action. In order to exist in this world, we must be able to take action on our own behalf, and awareness is an experience of simply being. It is consciousness that allows us to make changes and choices.

In the fields of self-help and personal growth, and especially in spiritual development, the "ego" can be seen as negative, something to rid ourselves of or to evolve beyond. But in this work, the ego is understood to be an absolute necessity and something integral to our stability.

Here, the ego is our "Primary Self System": the group of selves that oversees, operates, and manages our daily lives. Informed by our childhood and life experiences, the ego responds in the ways that we have developed to keep ourselves safe and have our needs met. Simply put, the ego is a group of selves that runs our lives and creates our personality. It is a naturally occurring process in human development, and it happens with little conscious involvement on our part.

Once we experience awareness, we can enact change through this group of selves. If our ego is our Primary Self System, then the "Aware Ego," as Hal and Sidra Stone have named it, is this same group of selves now having experienced awareness. Through separating from our primary selves and integrating our shadow sides, we can then experience an Aware Ego or the "Aware Ego Process." This is not a static experience or a point we finally arrive at. Becoming conscious is a dynamic process, constantly revealing, constantly evolving. This transformative process leads to conscious choice, which allows us to take action.

## THE ROLE OF THE INNER CHILD

Within each of us is a child — a child who is the combination of every age and of every developmental phase we have been through. Like the other selves, this child has distinct memories, ideas, and concerns. Although each age and developmental phase can be regarded as its own child, and so these interior states really make up a group of "children," we refer to them collectively as our "Inner Child." We might choose to name a specific Inner Child we are experiencing — my "Playful Child," for example, or my "Frightened Child" — or we might describe it as "the little girl I was when I was eight." The Inner Child, whether named or not, and whether we are conscious of it or not, represents our vulnerability. It represents our innocence, our sensitivity, our frailty, and our reliance upon others.

Being vulnerable is a powerful experience in our lives, defining who we are and how we behave. Our personalities develop in response to our vulnerability by finding the best ways possible to ensure our safety, protection, and care. We experience our vulnerability through our emotions and feelings. Our feelings are essential to our relationships, bringing connection and intimacy through empathy, compassion, and love. Because of these experiences, the Inner Child is at the core of our human experience, the core of our existence.

These childlike selves never grow up. They remain the age of the child they are within us. They don't change or mature, nor would we want them to. They bring richness, depth, and enjoyment to our lives. We have awe and wonder because they exist within us. Our job is not to "raise" them but to become aware that they exist and to care for them.

If they formed during a specific phase or out of a particular dramatic event in our lives, they carry the memories, perspectives, and the stories of our childhood at that time. They can also be more general — tied less to our personal childhoods — and carry the universal qualities of a child.

The Inner Child is a hidden gem within us and invariably shows up in our relationships; you could call it a cornerstone on our path of consciousness. Our Inner Child has gifts for our healing and can act as a guide that can lead us to what might be missing in our lives or relationships. Often, the Inner Child offers the best medicine for what ails us. By becoming aware of the Inner Child's existence and then consciously responding to its needs, we are healing our past, present, and future simultaneously.

Here is an example of an Inner Child bringing insight and healing. Beverly was suffering from fatigue. Although she was seeking treatment and alternative therapies, she was slow to recover and her progress was basically stalled. During a counseling session when Beverly wanted to discover if there were other reasons, other than physical, for this fatigue, she agreed to try Voice Dialogue work. The following is an excerpt of a conversation between Beverly and Gina:

GINA: Beverly, you've been suffering from some pretty extreme fatigue?

BEVERLY: Yes, terrible. I have no energy and can't even get through a day without feeling exhausted. I am feeling overwhelmed.

GINA: How is this affecting you and your life?

BEVERLY: Every area of my life is affected. I am withdrawn from my family and friends. My children exhaust me. I am resentful of my husband. It is very difficult.

GINA: Why don't we talk to the part of you that's feeling this exhaustion, this overwhelm?

[Beverly shifts her seat to her left.]

GINA: So you're the part of Beverly that is feeling exhausted? Pretty tired?

BEVERLY: Yes.

GINA: Tell me about this. What's going on?

BEVERLY: Well, she's so busy. She just does everything.

GINA: Beverly does?

BEVERLY: Yes.

GINA: Like what?

BEVERLY: She takes care of her mother, she takes care of her children, she takes care of her boss, she takes care of her husband, she takes care of her friends, and she takes care of her neighbors.

GINA: Wow, that is a lot of work! How does she take care of all of these people?

BEVERLY: She does *everything* for them. Her mom is not doing so great and needs a lot of care. She has a brother and sisters, and they could do it, but she just steps in and does it. She is extremely focused on her children and makes sure they have everything they need. She is always thinking about work and does everything for her boss. She even takes his calls on weekends and evenings. Every time anyone needs anything, they ask her, and she just does it.

GINA: That sounds really difficult for you. [Beverly nods.] You sound pretty young — can I ask — how old are you?

BEVERLY: Well, nine maybe?

GINA: I see. That is a lot to worry about for a nine-year-old. Is that the age when you came to be in Beverly's life? When she was nine years old?

[Beverly nods.]

GINA: What was going on for Beverly at that time?

BEVERLY: Well, her parents were arguing a lot. They were saying they were getting a divorce.

GINA: That is scary for a little girl.

BEVERLY: I thought if I was a good girl, then they would stop arguing.

GINA: Sweet girl. I can see that. That sounds frightening. How were you a good girl?

BEVERLY: I started to help my mom with chores. I was also really good at finding things that my dad lost, like keys or his papers for work. I helped a lot with my brother, too. I tried to make him behave so that Mommy and Daddy wouldn't fight.

Through this process, Beverly came to realize that she had held these feelings of responsibility, panic, and angst within her for all these years. She described being completely unconscious of her need to care for others as if she was on autopilot. For Beverly, part of bringing awareness to her process meant including her Inner Child, which perpetually acted as if it were nine years old and feeling the lack of control she once felt with her family.

Beverly saw this little girl as a part inside her that held these memories and experiences and lived like they were still happening today. She began to nurture that part of herself and parent her Inner Child by telling her she was loved and that it wasn't her job to worry about the adults. Those were big-people problems, and she was just a little girl. Once Beverly became conscious of this process, she could feel her little girl become anxious when someone needed help or was upset with her, or when her boss called her at home. When these feelings arose, she would soothe her child while at the same time making conscious choices about the best way to respond. In this way, she learned to heal the hurt she had experienced as a child and also take care of herself in the present.

As Beverly behaved differently in her life, she ultimately recovered from the exhaustion she was suffering. She set limits with her work and established boundaries with her boss, making conscious choices about the balance of her family and work lives based on what was most nurturing for her. She made a daily schedule for herself. She included playtime with her children and time for connecting with her husband as well as unstructured time where she could read, rest, or daydream. As she nurtured herself and her Inner Child, Beverly was more present for her friends and family. She and her husband reconnected and found the joy and intimacy they had been missing with each other. This is a good example of how the Inner Child can lead us to exactly what we need and bring healing to past, present, and future all at the same time.

In general, we usually remain unconscious of the process of the Inner Child and relatively unaware of our vulnerability. Although we may feel inadequate, insecure, or frightened at times, it is not the same as being in touch with our vulnerability. Nor does it allow us to consciously take care of our needs. Once we become aware of what we are feeling and recognize that our Inner Child is at the heart of what we are experiencing, we can make conscious choices about how to respond to its needs. We can take cues from our Inner Child as to what might be best in a given situation.

With this newfound awareness, we also discover the ways we have developed in an effort to care for the Inner Child. Sometimes we do this in ways that do not ultimately serve us, like ignoring or even burying the Inner Child as a way to protect it. The result is that we do not experience deep connections or intimacy, or we might feel alone or isolated. It can take time to reach or uncover our Inner Child, and to discover its many interior layers, but all we need to start is awareness: simply becoming aware that this process is going on inside us.

Our Inner Child touches our lives and all of our relationships. It's very common for us to unknowingly form an intimate relationship out of a need to care for our Inner Child. It feels so good, at first! Our partner loves us, they nurture us, they care for us, and maybe even pamper us. When we are feeling so loved in this way, it is often the Inner Child who is feeling this love and soaking it all in.

This is all very wonderful — until our partner has a bad day or is tired or distracted. If they are not able to be there for us, we suddenly feel rejected, ignored, or maybe not valued. We are hurt and blame them; all we see is what "they" have done wrong and how "they" have hurt us. It's as if we've taken our Inner Child and put them on the lap of someone else, expecting them to take care of us. It's no wonder we feel exposed, abandoned, or rejected! Once we become aware of what is happening within us — aware of the role of our Inner Child — we can shift our focus back to ourselves and our needs at the moment. We can stop looking to others to make us feel better, and we can act to do this for ourselves. Of course, it's appropriate to expect care and comfort from a partner, but no one, not even a parent, can anticipate or care for all of our needs. By recognizing our Inner Child when it arises, we learn to recognize our needs and the ways we can take care of ourselves.

# Exploring Common Selves

*In this chapter*, we will look at many of the archetypal selves that all people seem to possess. Each description includes a general overview of the self and examples of how it might be expressed or experienced in one's life. This is helpful for identifying selves within us, as well as seeing how those selves then relate to, and interact with, the people in our lives — especially the ones we are closest to.

There are selves that are not included here, of course, and you can learn more by reading Hal and Sidra Stone's excellent books. The selves identified in this section will be particularly helpful for times when we are experiencing difficulty in a relationship or feeling stuck in certain areas of our lives. Reading through the descriptions can spark insight into what might be happening on a subconscious level, or it might help us to identify an area in our lives where we are experiencing an imbalance.

## Rule Maker

The Rule Maker is the part of us that creates and carries out the rules that we live by. It is so basic to our personality that we don't even know it is there and operating. It is informed by the values of our family and culture, as well as by our primary selves and what is important to those selves. If, maybe because of our family or upbringing, we feel it is very important to have a pleasing personality, the Rule Maker will make rules about how we should behave in order to always be pleasing to others.

In addition to defining how we should behave, the Rule Maker determines the guidelines for the choices, large and small, that determine how we live our lives. Right and wrong are big issues for the Rule Maker, and it has strong feelings and opinions about these.

In our relationships, the Rule Maker determines our role, how we should act, what is acceptable or not, as well as how we should be treated, how others should act toward us, and what roles they should be fulfilling. (The Rule Maker is very fond of the word "should.") The Rule Maker can affect our ability to be intimate with our partners because we can get stuck in a certain role or way of being, rather than having access to a more authentic experience in the moment. If one person's Rule Maker is very authoritarian, that can polarize the other person to be rebellious, and this of course seriously affects the dynamics of a relationship.

Most commonly, the Rule Maker makes rules for our well-being. Although the rules can feel restrictive, the Rule Maker's intention is to keep us safe, emotionally and physically. We all have some version of a Rule Maker, and if our childhood was particularly turbulent or unstable, our Rule Maker might be quite rigid and strong. If a person was raised in a family with authoritarian parents, the person might develop "rules" about being free flowing, or they could be defiant and rebellious in opposition to their parents. Alternatively, they may feel that unquestioning obedience is the only safe path open to them.

As with all of the selves, the healing we need to bring balance to our lives and to our relationships is to recognize our Rule Maker and value it for doing a specific job. As we begin our consciousness work, we learn new ways to care for others and ourselves, and we discover new ways to bring greater balance into our lives and our relationships.

Opposite selves to the Rule Maker can be shadow sides for us, or they could be selves carried in our partners — these opposite selves can include a rebel, an easygoing self, "being" energy, and a spontaneous, free spirit. In some cases, the Rule Maker may decide you must be a free spirit all the time, and so you develop a counterculture identity or regularly oppose external authority or the rules of society.

## SPIRITUAL RULE MAKER

A Spiritual or New Age Rule Maker develops once a person starts on a path of consciousness or personal growth. Similar selves can include a "Recovery Rule Maker," who sets rigid rules for a person once they begin a path of recovery or a twelve-step program, and a "Religious Rule Maker," who adopts rules as espoused by a religious tradition or as influenced by a conversion experience.

The Spiritual Rule Maker starts out as an effort to seek answers, alleviate pain, recover from addiction, explore deeper meaning in our lives, and/or find our greater purpose, but it evolves into defining new rules that replace the previous ones we felt bound by. The New Age or Spiritual Rule Maker adopts these new ideas and forms a new set of commands on how to live based on these new values.

The flaw in identifying with these Rule Makers is that we remain locked into rigid, limited ways of living. Too often, we become oppressed rather than finding freedom. Some common "New Age" rules, for example, are to always be happy, to always be forgiving, to accept every situation, to always be grateful, and to be kind and loving toward everyone at all times.

These can be excellent principles, goals, or aspirations. However, we cannot be these things all the time, especially in our relationships. If my partner hurts my feelings, and I am identified with my Spiritual Rule Maker, I may feel I cannot express myself honestly. Instead, I require myself to be kind, understanding, and forgiving, or perhaps see this situation as having happened on purpose so I can learn from it. When I can't be honest with my partner, I lose intimacy, and our relationship's aliveness or authentic connection suffers. To experience genuine intimacy, we have to learn how to disagree with each other, express our differences, and reason things out safely and respectfully.

It's important to note that someone new in recovery often must make drastic changes to their behavior, lifestyle, friends, or environment. They must establish new habits and boundaries for themselves, and so they may identify with a strong Recovery Rule Maker for this reason. However, as above, a person in recovery should avoid what might be called "emotional rules," such as that they can never feel a negative feeling, that they must always feel grateful, or that they can't admit a craving out of fear that it will tarnish their recovery. Rules like these may set the person up to return to their old form of addiction. A healthy and natural balance can be to accept and express what we are experiencing, while at the same time using the tools of recovery or working the twelve steps. As with the other selves, problems arise when we don't make conscious choices but are locked into only one way of being.

## PUSHER

The Pusher is a power self, a driving force pushing us to get things done, to do more, even to be a certain way *all* the time. Its job is to accomplish everything that we want to do. The Pusher carries what we call "doing" energy. It is the self that wakes us up first thing in the morning and writes out our to-do lists for the day. The Pusher packs in a daily schedule full of tasks, phone calls, and errands.

The Pusher works in partnership with the Rule Maker and the Perfectionist. It carries out what we determine our "rules" to be and pushes us to achieve our goals or the goals of the Perfectionist. A person with a strong Pusher might be described as a "Type A" personality or as "very driven." The Pusher is a huge force in our culture and is often overvalued in our work environments. It always wants to be accomplishing, producing, and focusing on "deliverables."

A person with a strong Pusher will be driven in their relationships as well, often organizing time together and making sure to be always "doing" things and keeping busy without much downtime. They are more likely to be planning a packed schedule and less likely to be spontaneous or go with the flow, even on a lazy Sunday morning.

They may also be driven to work on their relationships, wanting to "process" often, and constantly wanting to dig deeper or make a better connection during time together. They often push their partner to change, to be different, to act in another way. This can be tiresome and challenging for the partner — though a strong Pusher is often in a relationship with a Caretaker or Pleaser who goes along willingly (at least for a while!).

Opposites of the Pusher will generally be selves with "being" energy at their core, selves that value resting, relaxing, taking time, being in nature, and connecting with others. Creative and expressive selves, as well as intuitive or spontaneous selves, can also be opposite energies to the Pusher. A person with a strong Pusher will likely be in relationship with a person who has at least some of these opposite qualities. Often, someone with a strong Pusher interacts with others and prefers being out in the world, while their partner is more of a homebody or prefers more contemplative time to themselves.

## Spiritual Pusher

A Spiritual or New Age Pusher blends the qualities of both the Spiritual Rule Maker and the Pusher. Although we sometimes use the term "New Age," this self adopts whatever religious, recovery, or spiritual principles the person has identified as appropriate, valuable, and the "right" way to be. Whatever the terms, the Spiritual Pusher becomes driven to achieve those spiritual goals.

It is important to a good Spiritual Pusher to read more, to learn more, to grow more, and to essentially become more "spiritual." Someone with a strong Spiritual Pusher might have inspirational books piled up beside their bed and are actively reading all of them, of course! They regularly sign up for classes, workshops, and retreats; they always want to be learning new tools and techniques for experiencing personal growth and ultimately greater awareness, consciousness, and enlightenment.

Someone with a strong Spiritual or New Age Pusher is often in relationship with someone else who has a strong Spiritual Pusher. They may attend workshops together, listen to speakers, and share books. If one partner doesn't have a strong Spiritual Pusher, however, it can be difficult and annoying for them, since they will most likely be pestered to read a book, listen to an excerpt, or be dragged begrudgingly to hear the next famous author who comes to town.

Opposites of a New Age or Spiritual Pusher are similar to the opposites of all varieties of Pushers; they include selves that are relaxed and easygoing, spontaneous, creative, and expressive. Regarding the "spiritual" selves, opposites may include selves focused on earthly matters, such as one's environment, physical appearance, body, finances, or work life. Opposites can also include certain intellectual selves, along with rational, pragmatic, or linear thinking selves. Generally, we find that the emotional selves and childlike selves can carry an opposite energy to "spiritual" selves as well.

## PERFECTIONIST

The goal of the Perfectionist self is to have us be at our best at all times so that we are loved, admired, and valued. The Perfectionist makes sure we are doing everything perfectly, that is, according to its standards. Unfortunately, the Perfectionist has such high standards that it is impossible and unrealistic to live up to them. The Perfectionist works in partnership with the Rule Maker and the Pusher: the Rule Maker makes the rules, the Perfectionist makes sure they are carried out exactly, and the Pusher makes sure they are carried out all the time. The Inner Critic is also part of this team — it is like a yappy dog constantly nipping at you, or herding you, to keep you on track.

The Perfectionist has strong ideas about what is acceptable, both for ourselves and others. The Perfectionist wants things done in whatever way it perceives as right, proper, or good, depending on the situation or circumstance. The Perfectionist is informed by other selves, who help define what these "gold standards" are, and then it's the Perfectionist's sole job to make sure we achieve and maintain them — all of them!

The Perfectionist is active in several aspects of our relationships; it focuses on making sure we are perfect, our partner is perfect, and the relationship itself is perfect. Someone with a strong Perfectionist might believe in and create an imaginary picture of the "perfect relationship," and then constantly compare where their relationship is to where it should or needs to be. With a deeply rooted Perfectionist, there is no room for error or even for a learning curve. If there is a conflict, someone with a strong Perfectionist may have difficulty admitting to or taking responsibility for a mistake or being able to genuinely hear their partner's criticisms or perspective. This might challenge their ideas of who they are and how they should act, and that is difficult for them to tolerate. The Perfectionist might become so focused on finding the perfect partner that the person ends up staying single, since no one they meet can live up to their unrealistic expectations.

Because a strong Perfectionist is such a powerful energy, the opposite energies are usually equally strong. This can easily create tension in a relationship if there is no consciousness about these polarities within us. Opposites that can bring tension to a relationship can be the energies of a Rebel or a Procrastinator, or someone who is withdrawn or apathetic. A partner might express other opposite energies, such as going with the flow and being spontaneous, whimsical, adventurous, and willing to make mistakes!

## INNER CRITIC AND JUDGE

At its best, the Inner Critic is a discerning voice within us that helps us to think critically, navigate decision-making, evaluate situations, avoid mistakes, and ultimately be the best we can be. Sounds supportive, right? What the Inner Critic actually sounds like, however, is a running commentary on everything we are doing, telling us how we could be doing it better, pointing out our mistakes — all too often — and picking on us, needling us, and driving us to improve, be better, work faster, and so on. At its worst, the Inner Critic can become a relentless onslaught of negativity that makes us feel terrible.

The Inner Critic and the Judge are essentially two sides of the same coin. One is inwardly critical of ourselves, and the other is outwardly judgmental of others. When we realize we have a judgment about something, we have surely found one of our disowned selves — or a primary self, as the case may be. As we've seen, we can use this realization to bring awareness to the parts of ourselves we might be overidentified with and to the parts we are not allowing or have enough of in our lives.

The intention of the Inner Critic is actually to protect us, to take care of us, and to keep us safe, both physically and emotionally. Its aim is to keep us out of harm's way, to avoid painful disappointment or the displeasure of others, and to help us avoid criticism — by doing so well that no one else can criticize us.

People with strong Inner Critics were often influenced during childhood by someone who was critical of them, usually overly so. This could be a critical parent, an older sibling, or some other central figure in their early lives. This adult or authority figure may have also had a large or overactive Inner Critic and passed on its fear, insecurity, and anxiety.

If we aren't aware of our Inner Critic, we may think that this is just the way we talk to ourselves. We don't even recognize its constant commentary. Once we have awareness of this part of ourselves — once we realize that it is in fact just one part among many other selves — we can begin to experience some ease in our lives. We can breathe deeply more often and relax occasionally.

Once we have this awareness, healing begins, and we start making conscious choices and finding balance in our lives. The best way we have found to deal with our Inner Critic is simply to say, "Thank you for sharing," or "I hear you, and I will give your input some thought." This helps to neutralize any intensity and immediately shifts the energy so that another, more balanced voice or self can come in.

Opposites of the Inner Critic tend to be selves that are more carefree, easygoing, or spontaneous. A partner in relationship with someone who has a strong Inner Critic will likely carry these energies. However, a partner in relationship with someone who has a strong Inner Critic can also be outwardly critical toward their partner (a Judge), and this supports and perpetuates the beliefs of their partner's Inner Critic.

## PROTECTOR / CONTROLLER

The Protector/Controller is at the helm — in the driver's seat, really — of our inner group of primary selves and is the guiding force of our ego or personality. Its "job" begins at birth when we are vulnerable and totally reliant upon those around us. The Protector/Controller assesses our environment and our caregivers and determines the best way for us to behave so that we have our needs met and are emotionally and physically safe. As we grow and develop, the Protector/Controller reinforces the aspects of the primary selves that develop within us. Similar to the Rule Maker, the Protector/Controller does this by establishing rules so that we avoid anything that is potentially harmful — and in doing so, we can end up becoming overly restrictive. It is very cautious about doing or trying new things and may keep us from taking risks or experimenting.

In general, the Protector will gradually let go of its control when it feels we are taking proper responsibility for ourselves. The Protector is a responsive self and reacts, or is activated, based on the level of threat we experience. The more dramatic our childhood and formative years, the more intense this response will be. The less dramatic our early experiences, the more neutral this aspect will be and the more ease we will feel in our day-to-day lives.

Everyone has a Protector/Controller, and it can be experienced in different ways in relationships. For example, if one has a strong Caregiver, then the Protector/Controller will make sure that the Caregiver does its job very well; we care for and always think of others so that we do not get rejected and are never abandoned. This can go beyond a need to take care of others and become a safety mechanism. Understanding this dynamic is very helpful in unpacking conflict or arguments with others, especially when we feel frustrated and stuck. When we recognize our partner's Protector/Controller, we can see that they are not trying to control us, ultimately, but rather they need to have a sense of control within themselves.

The Protector/Controller can also come up in therapy or during facilitation (as we'll see in that chapter), acting as a gatekeeper. One way this is experienced is when a person feels hesitant about what they are being asked to do or talk about, and they are guarded or difficult to connect with. If this happens, whether in a therapeutic setting or in a conversation with a dear friend, helpful ways to diffuse the tension or soften the need for protection is to ask: "Are you feeling hesitant right now?" "What are you feeling right now?" or "What are you concerned might happen?" Sometimes this self can be put at ease once it has a chance to voice its concerns out loud, and you are able to listen to and honor its concerns.

If a sense of resistance persists, it may be best to leave the conversation for a while and try again later. Keep in mind that the Protector/Controller is acting this way for a reason, following a specific rule. There is probably another self that it needs to protect or it feels vulnerable.

## Responsible and Competent Selves

The Responsible Self is the part of us that takes complete responsibility for different areas in our lives. It makes sure that everything that needs to be done gets done. It manages our commitments, makes appointments, and follows through on all of our tasks. It double-checks our to-do lists and gets us pointed in the right direction every morning.

The Competent self is closely related to the Responsible self, so much so that we put them together almost interchangeably. A

Competent self is super-capable at everything, gets many things done, and does them all well. There is a quality of achievement with both of these aspects, as they are inherently goal-oriented and value success and recognition. "Good job!" is music to the ears of any good Responsible and Competent self.

These selves see when things need to be done and when things have not been done properly. They take responsibility for many areas outside of our own lives and are likely to get involved with projects, take on commitments, and work on committees or with community groups. They make excellent volunteers!

People with strong Responsible and Competent selves are reliable and find roles in their relationships and work lives where they are the ones who are depended upon. It can be lovely to be in relationship with someone who has a strong Responsible and Competent self. They do all the planning, they make sure things get done, they organize trips, and they complete household projects. They are also likely to be the ones that make the medical appointments, keep the family calendar, and pay the bills. The partner with the strong Responsible self will often take complete responsibility for the relationship as well, bringing attention to what might need to be worked on or improved.

When there is too much of an imbalance, however, both partners can end up feeling resentful. The person with the strong Responsible and Competent self can feel like their partner is "lazy," not doing enough, or not caring enough. In return, their partner can feel suffocated or controlled by the other's well-intentioned decision-making or irritated by their always knowing everything and doing everything so well. An overactive Responsible and Competent self will tend to take over their partner's life, managing what they do and telling them how they should do it — and this, of course, is generally not very appreciated by their partner!

Since Responsible and Competent selves carry "doing" energy, the opposite selves carry "being" energy, which can be experienced as both positive and negative. The positive side is carefree, easygoing, relaxed, spontaneous, creative, emotional, and sensitive. The negative side is irresponsible, underachieving, withdrawn, apathetic, rebellious, and lacking effort and initiative. When there is an imbalance in a relationship with someone who has a strong Responsible and Competent self, the key (as it is with all selves) is to recognize this overidentification and embrace the opposite energies that are appropriate for the given situation.

If our partner is feeling "smothered" by us, for example, we can take a step back and allow them more ownership and freedom in the situation. If we are telling ourselves we "always have to be the one to do everything," we could let our partners do things in their own ways and take time to focus on our own needs or on nurturing ourselves.

## RATIONALIST AND KNOWER

In the Psychology of Selves, we define the Rationalist as the part of us that is always thinking, analyzing, interpreting. The job of this self is to understand as much as possible about how things work and to assess and learn from the people, situations, and world around us. The Rationalist self can be a brilliant gift and an incredible tool, vital to our existence and our very survival. We refer to it as the "Rationalist" because its evaluations and responses are rational, linear, pragmatic, impersonal, well thought through, and properly analyzed. The Rationalist is a common primary self, especially in the Western world, where such an approach to life is highly valued and coveted.

A closely related self is the "Knower." While its function is to understand and analyze, it is also confident in what it knows. Someone with a strong Knower can become quite self-righteous. The Knower knows about life in general as well as all the answers to any specific questions that might come up. This self can manifest in various areas of our lives, including the psychological and spiritual.

A Psychological Knower analyzes people and relationships in particular. The Psychological Knower sees into the motivations of a person (usually involving their partner or the person they are in conflict with); this self analyzes someone's "story" and how it affects them and their relationships.

A Spiritual Knower knows the "truth" about spiritual or religious beliefs for itself, and it knows what is right for everyone else, too. Since the Knower always "knows," it is also always "right" — having the right answers, knowing the right way, knowing the "true" feelings and inner workings of the person they are analyzing. It is easy to tell when someone's Knower is active because they speak in absolutes and make absolute statements — "You are feeling *this*," and "You always/never do *that*...." A Knower always believes its perspective is "true" and "right."

Like all the other selves, our Rationalist and Knower are trying to help us or keep us safe by "knowing." They never want us to be in a situation where we are unprepared, and they perceive that "not knowing" makes us vulnerable to criticism, failure, embarrassment, and rejection. The Rationalist also wants to be sure we are safe and well cared for, analyzing every situation and weighing all our options so that we can make the best decision possible. The Rationalist and Knower have many gifts that are good and valuable. Without these aspects, we would not be able to navigate through life.

The Rationalist and Knower don't really understand emotions or people who are governed more by emotions, more by "feeling" than by "knowing." These people might be described by the Rationalist and Knower as "emotional." Being analytical, the Rationalist refers to emotions in an intellectual context and intellectualizes the feelings of others. They know what *they think* their partner is feeling but not with their own feelings or compassion. When one person is overidentified with their Rationalist and Knower selves and the other is trying to explain how they feel or why their feelings are hurt, this makes for a difficult conversation, often leading into an argument. The Rationalist and Knower will tend to minimize or dismiss the feelings of the other person because they can't understand or relate to their feelings. In this scenario, the partner will often feel unheard and possibly "wrong" to be having these feelings.

This example makes it clear why understanding the various selves can help us not only understand our own reactions but also those of other people. We need to explore each of these selves, including those that are the "opposite," in order to better explain our feelings and have compassion for others. If we overidentify with our Rationalist and Knower selves, we should take care to experience the emotional self that represents the opposite of that approach.

When we are overidentified with the Rationalist and Knower, we overvalue thinking and intellectual processing. This can keep us from experiencing other aspects of life, especially intimacy in our relationships. We experience intimacy through our feelings, emotions, vulnerability, and humility. If we are always "knowing," we are most likely not listening, and listening is a vital key to fulfilling relationships.

Experiences like creativity or spontaneity are also difficult for us when we are identified with our Rationalist. The Rationalist tends to analyze the right way to do something rather than letting a creative process flow or allowing a mistake to unfold into a work of art. A spontaneous activity could be counter to the Rationalist's way of planning, thinking through, or analyzing the options.

Opposites of the Rationalist and Knower are generally "being" selves, including the selves that are connected to our emotions and intuition, creative and expressive selves, and spontaneous, free-spirited selves. These selves hold the key to bringing balance to our lives when we find we are overidentified with our Rationalist. The energies of these selves are often carried in or expressed through our partners, family, and even coworkers when we have a Rationalist and Knower as a primary self.

## PLEASER AND CARETAKER

The Pleaser is the part of us who finds absolute joy in pleasing others. It is totally focused on other people and wants to make them happy. The Pleaser can be very intuitive, even hypervigilant, in assessing how a person is and the best way for us to act around them or behave in a given situation. They are also very good at grasping what is expected of us and making sure we fulfill these expectations so that others are pleased with us and our work. The Pleaser has a passive quality, responding to others or taking its cues from others versus initiating its own agenda.

The Caretaker is a self that is also focused on others. The Caretaker wants to make certain those around us are well taken care of and that their needs are being met. The Caretaker looks ahead, anticipating needs that might arise and even tending to them before the other person even knows what they need! It takes care of all types of tasks, chores, and responsibilities for others. The Caretaker is also very nurturing: nursing those who are sick, helping those in need, and being sensitive to those who are hurting. The Pleaser and the Caretaker overlap in so many ways that they are inseparable, and we generally work with them together.

The Pleaser and the Caretaker want to make sure we are liked, and they are motivated by appreciation and approval from others. They feel so good when they are recognized or acknowledged for their efforts. These selves become highly attuned to other people's feelings and emotions. They exist to please and serve.

Being attuned to others' needs and feelings, they are also sensitive to the displeasure and disappointment of others. They are accommodating and never want to have a disagreement or let someone down. They cannot tolerate conflict or discord. The worst thing for a Pleaser and Caretaker is when someone thinks they did something wrong or is upset with them. The Pleaser and Caretaker are solely focused on other people's happiness and do not account for what we *ourselves* might need or want. They don't consider if a situation works for us or not.

When in a relationship, the Pleaser and Caretaker want to take care of their partner so their partner will be happy. A strong Pleaser and Caretaker will often like whatever their partner likes and do whatever their partner does. This can feel good to others. People enjoy, and feel loved, when someone focuses on their needs and gives them attention. When the Pleaser and Caretaker selves are out of balance, however, the attention can feel overbearing, even suffocating. The underlying motivation of a strong Pleaser and Caretaker is to have their partner love them, not reject them, and to never leave them. But intense caretaking can disempower their partner, disallowing them the freedom to take care of themselves.

Someone with a strong Pleaser and Caretaker might find that they feel lost in the relationship and struggle to take care of themselves and their own needs. They might not even know they have needs! When you have a strong Pleaser and Caretaker, you can't have any contrary thoughts, feelings, or beliefs because you don't want to experience conflict or risk having someone get upset with you. Commonly, someone with a strong Pleaser and Caretaker will often get sick, be fatigued, or experience migraines and tension headaches from stress. Because their primary focus is on others, the message the Pleaser and Caretaker send is that it is selfish to do something for yourself or it is indulgent to take time to do something that makes you happy. We are left with a feeling of being stuck and unhappy.

This is where the opposite selves can be so helpful! The first step in finding balance is to be aware that the Pleaser and Caretaker are selves. Yes, we might be thoughtful and kind, but if we feel stuck — if we feel obligated to be nice and take care of others all the time — then these selves are running the show. Once we recognize this, other energies flow in almost immediately.

The opposites of a Pleaser and Caretaker usually have qualities of self-interest and self-care. When a person is locked into the Pleaser and Caretaker selves, they see self-care as selfish. Very often, the person blames their partner for being selfish and self-centered as well. With consciousness, we see that it is actually nurturing and helpful to focus on ourselves, so that we can recharge and ultimately have more to give!

Other opposite qualities may include being a straight talker and a boundary setter; people may emphasize a more removed or impersonal self or a more introverted and quiet self. These qualities are often what the partner carries when in relationship with a strong Pleaser and Caretaker.

## FAMILIAL SELF — GOOD PARENT, CHILD, SIBLING

We have so many "good" selves within us — selves that want to take care of others, nurture others, provide for others, and please others. When these selves are expressed with a familial quality, we refer to them by the type of familial role they embody. A parental quality of looking after or watching over is referred to as "Good Mother" or "Good Father." When this self is expressed with a quality of listening, following directions, and serving, we refer to it as "Good Daughter" or "Good Sister" and "Good Son" or "Good Brother." We identify these titles by the person's gender. We have these selves within us no matter what our actual familial relationships — that is, we don't need to be a parent to possess a "Good Mother" self. Also, we have these selves in all of our relationships whether we are interacting with blood relatives or not.

Here's an example: We have already discussed the Caretaker, a self that takes care of the needs of others, both physically and emotionally. When a woman with a strong "Good Mother" is caretaking, she blends her caretaking with a quality of tenderness, of loving kindness, or a sense of doting, the way a mother would. Someone who is overidentified with her "Good Mother" might shift from kindness to being controlling and manipulative, and her attempts at managing other people's lives can feel suffocating to the recipient of their caring.

A "Good Father" is a man who provides for his family or team or who operates under the belief that it is his role and duty to take care of those around him. A person overidentified with his "Good Father" might take on a disproportionate amount of responsibility for others and can come across as rigid and forceful.

A Good Daughter/Son or Good Sister/Brother acts out of obedience or duty. They believe they are doing the right thing by following the directions, rules, and guidance of parents or bosses. They might not challenge or speak out against anyone they perceive to be above them or in a position of authority. Their intention is to serve and follow directions as well as nurture and appreciate those caring and providing for them. Most often, the Good Parent self in one person is in relationship with the Good Child of another. This can happen in family relations as well as at work and in intimate partnerships.

One example of this in a work scenario is where someone who is a supervisor might have a "Good Father" as a primary self. He takes care of everyone and makes sure they are happy. He is also focused on the team and works hard to ensure that everyone is successful. He makes sure his staff is compensated well, and although he is focused on results, he wants to make sure that everyone is reaching their individual goals as well. Some of his employees will likely have strong "Good Child" selves. They make sure he receives his reports the way he likes, they think of things before he even asks for them, and they are thoughtful in the planning of his schedule and appointments. They feel proud to serve him and care for him, and in return they are appreciated and paid well. This relationship is simply an exchange between these selves of caretaking and caring with a strong sense of duty.

These patterns often work very well in families and workplaces. But these patterns don't work very well when, for instance, a "Good Daughter" feels like she doesn't have a choice and cannot speak up or express her needs, or when she is afraid to break the rules or disappoint those she serves. A "Good Father" might feel inadequate if he cannot provide for his family in the way he thinks he should. He may feel like a disappointment to his wife's "Good Daughter" self. A "Good Mother" might become demanding and critical of her husband. A "Good Son" might feel rejected or feel as if he is falling short of expectations.

Like all of the selves, these selves serve us — they take care of us, keep us safe, and help us care for those around us. When out of balance, though, they can become restrictive or binding, limiting our intimacy and experience of joy. Often, the key to lightening the grip of an overbearing "Good Family" member is to turn our attention within and nurture ourselves, be a good parent to ourselves, validate our own feelings, and feel good about the work we are doing and how we do it. By nurturing ourselves, we fill ourselves up, and we lessen the need to be cared for by others or to care for them from a place of lack or anxiety.

## AUTHORITARIAN AND REBEL

The Authoritarian and Rebel are opposite selves that form two sides of the same coin. We usually put them together because they are inseparable in some ways. They often reflect the same internal process, one that we project to the outside world. If someone has a strong Rebel as a primary self, they most likely have an adverse reaction to rules, authority, teachers, lawmakers, law enforcement, or people they perceive as controlling, mothering, or managing. They want to be independent, freethinking, and adventurous, and they don't want to conform or be restricted or bound by anyone's rules. A person with a strong Rebel was most likely raised by someone with an Authoritarian primary self or within a controlling environment. They might have had parents who were micromanaging and smothering or who were disciplinarians or even abusive. At some point, they felt controlled, stifled, and powerless, and their solution for escaping the dominance of the other person was to react negatively and seize control of their own life, relying only on themselves and following their own ideas and direction.

A person with a strong Authoritarian self is someone who has definite rules for behaving and a strong sense of right and wrong — especially where others are concerned. They also have expectations of those around them that they should follow rules, take direction, or behave according to the Authoritarian's beliefs. This is similar to some other archetypal selves, such as the Rule Maker, the Knower, and the Inner Critic. A person with a Rebel or Authoritarian as a primary self is most likely overidentified with these other archetypes as well and uses them to reinforce their ideas and what they think is right.

The reason we see these selves as two sides of the same coin is because, if you project a strong Rebel self out to the world, you most likely have a strong Authoritarian self active inside — whether you are aware of this voice or not. Most often, an internalized voice is telling the person what to do, how they should be, and what is right or wrong, and the person is not allowed to do anything outside of the "norm" as defined by this voice. The person acting as the Rebel is often attempting to dominate or control, and they also feel controlled by the Rebel self, which reinforces its rules through internal messages it runs all the time. Back in the days of audiocassettes, we called this the "tape that was playing in your head" (and before that, the "broken record that keeps playing over and over"). Ultimately, the Rebel self is an internal voice telling a person to behave a certain way, as opposed to a person being told this by another person or external command.

A person with a strong Authoritarian inevitably encounters the Rebel in others. As they exert their will and ideas or power over other people, others retaliate or push back. This only makes an Authoritarian self stronger, digging their heels in with more force. Like the Authoritarian inside a Rebel, the Rebel is on the inside of the Authoritarian, in cooperation with the Inner Critic and other archetypal selves. The Rebel self that is on the inside — even though it's usually disowned — is challenging the ideas, authority, and power of the Authoritarian primary self. The more self-doubt there is inside, the stronger the Authoritarian self exerts its will on the outside.

It is important to note that a reactive Rebel or a controlling Authoritarian do not necessarily act out in an aggressive manner. Withholding, ignoring, or dismissing are also ways that both the Rebel and the Authoritarian act out. They can both be passive-aggressive, competitive, and manipulative. Sometimes they act out in overt ways, but very often they are more subtle in their reactions and behaviors.

# Integration:
# Awareness and Attention

*The most important reason* to work with disowned selves is so that we can make conscious choices in our life. If I am locked into only one way of being in the world or of handling a situation, then I am stuck in a default position and severely limited in my responses and options. Once I can access all the different parts of myself, I can make a conscious choice about how to handle a situation or make a decision. I am open to bringing in ideas from the different selves, as if I am consulting with a wise group of friends that all have my best interests at heart.

Once we experience talking with these selves, we can see how these selves work together, and we can explore what is disowned for us and what might be a primary self for us. With awareness, we can shift the grip these selves have on our lives, and this influences the actions we take.

Once we realize that it is our own internal voice that is telling us to behave in a certain way or to follow certain rules, we can lessen our knee-jerk reactions to people or situations. We can address the fear within us that is triggering feelings of insecurity or inadequacy. When we start to see which selves have been primary in our lives, that awareness itself helps us to separate from these selves. Once we can separate from our primary selves, we can experience other energies that we have been cut off from. We can find renewed intimacy in our relationships through a sense of peace and balance that comes from acknowledging and embracing all of the other selves within us.

When we start embracing all of ourselves, we are led into the powerful inner work of integrating our shadow selves into the fullness of our lives. Even though these energies have been disowned in our lives, they often are not buried or inactive, but instead they influence us and cause all sorts of problems in our lives.

If an aspect is unknown to us, we often feel deep relief when we access this energy and experience it more and more in our lives. However, we have disowned many aspects because of the pain associated with them. Often we were hurt by expressing them, or we were ostracized or rejected, and this means we need to be gentle, patient, and kind with ourselves when we bring our shadow selves into the light of our awareness.

Practicing separation from the primary ways we are in the world allows us to more readily access these energies. It takes practice to embrace these energies within us. The key is to keep the intention in mind that we are creating the space for their expression in our lives and in our relationships.

Learning about the selves brings us greater awareness, and this awareness is the first step in becoming conscious. I often find that participants in my workshops come with the idea that becoming conscious is a huge undertaking and serious — maybe even painful — work. Or they may come from a tradition in which becoming conscious involves silent meditation and contemplative prayer with a transcendent quality. I had some of these ideas before embracing this work. Now my understanding of becoming conscious involves simply, and profoundly, becoming aware of what is going on within us at the moment — and, in doing so, we become aware of who we are.

To do so, we take a nonjudgmental, open-minded view and simply observe what motivates us, how we act, and what we feel, and then we inquire where these ideas and behaviors come from. As we listen, learn, and accept these truths we discover about ourselves, we develop a foundation to build upon. We can decide what serves us or what might be holding us back. We can use the tools in this book to celebrate who we are and to have compassion for who we are. With our growing awareness, we can make conscious choices about who we are and how we want to be in our relationships and in the world.

## LISTENING TO OURSELVES

As we learn more about the different selves within us, the first step to becoming conscious of them is to listen to ourselves with awareness. We can hear in our own voice (as we talk not only to others but to ourselves) the ideas, behaviors, attitudes, and judgments of these selves, and we can recognize when these selves are interacting with people in our lives. We can also learn to recognize what they sound like and what they say. Then, when we catch ourselves using specific words or phrases, we can tell that a certain self or part of us is speaking.

This is particularly noticeable when we are complaining or arguing. For example, we might hear ourselves say, or think, "This place is such a mess! They never pick up their things! I always have to clean up!" Especially when we use the words "never" and "always," we know right away that a "self" is ranting. When we are speaking through a self, it is usually one-sided and always right, of course! We tend to speak in absolutes and make declarations or demands. There is no balance when we are speaking from a primary self.

When we come from a place of consciousness, however, we can see different sides to a situation and come across in a more neutral way. With consciousness, we also have insight into what is happening within us, and this allows us to balance our perspective.

Our ability to communicate improves dramatically once we begin this work. We have access to the different parts within us, and this allows us to have empathy and understanding when listening to another person, particularly someone we are close to. We also have more awareness about how we are behaving or why we might be acting a certain way. This allows us to be more balanced in our communications.

The most critical aspect to becoming conscious of "who" is speaking, then, is to listen to yourself. I love the phrase, "It's not what you say. It's who says it!" For instance, even if we have a valid point to make, if we speak from our primary self, this point will likely sound like it's judging the other person, and it will not be received so well. If we have a Responsible and Competent primary self, it will likely be judgmental of those around us when they are not being responsible or competent (according to our Responsible self). A mother might say to her child, "Could you please clean your room?" But what the child hears — because of her gestures, tone, and expressions — is, "Your room is a disaster! You're a lazy, irresponsible child to live like that." Without the mother's realizing it, her primary self is judging her child for not cleaning his room. She comes across as a controlling and critical mother, and most often a child will adopt an opposite self and act out in response or criticize her in retaliation.

If the mother can listen to herself with awareness, she can hear what is happening within her. Perhaps the mother came home stressed, is feeling overwhelmed, or maybe she has not been asking for help and is feeling powerless. She has blamed her child for not being helpful, but she now realizes that what she needs to do is to ask for help so she can take better care of herself. With this new awareness, she can communicate to her child from this place, "I'm sorry. I'm not angry with you, but I need a little extra help today. Could you please straighten up your room before dinner?"

## TALKING WITH THE SELVES

Discovering what is motivating us — what is actually moving us in a certain direction — and creating awareness about what might be holding us back, even "sabotaging" us, is at the heart of this work with selves. Listing the traits we are most comfortable with and the opposites of those characteristics is a helpful way to start this process. It gives us a peek into who we are and who we have the potential to become.

Ultimately, to discover and experience these aspects as selves and give voice to these feelings inside us, we use a technique we call "facilitation." Facilitation is a practice of interviewing a self — in which we actually sit and talk with this self and learn about its thoughts, priorities, concerns, and tasks at hand. By shifting our perspective to that of this self, we experience what the energy of this self feels like in our body and what we feel like when we are thinking and acting on the initiatives of this self. This process helps us to recognize when a particular self is running the show and we have become a bystander in our own life.

When we get in touch with our inner process and have access to the different aspects within us, our communication becomes balanced and authentic. In part 4, we will look more thoroughly at how to use facilitation and other tools for developing our relationships.

# Couples: The Special Role of Romantic Partnerships

*Throughout this book* we have discussed many types of relationships, not just romantic partnerships. However, many of us are on a path of striving for greater intimacy or creating a deeper connection with our partner. In this chapter, I wanted to address specific aspects of romantic couple relationships.

Let's look first at how a romantic relationship often unfolds. What happens? Sometimes we find ourselves attracted to a person who is very different from us. We may feel drawn to someone "across a crowded room." We may not even know exactly why we chose this person. It may be love at first sight, or it may be a gradual shifting from a friendship to a romantic partnership. Sometimes, we have an opposite reaction to someone. We may feel dislike or irritation at first, but eventually those impressions change, and qualities we once rejected might become attractive. In any case, however they develop, these strong feelings of attraction lead us to want to be closer to this person.

When we find ourselves deeply drawn to someone, and we allow ourselves to get closer, our romantic feelings may get stronger, and we may experience that most delicious and delightful feeling of falling in love. When this happens, the primary selves, such as the Protector, Perfectionist, and Pusher, feel that all is well and that they can loosen their hold on our life a little bit. The Inner Child feels loved, accepted, and taken care of by all the attention the couple is giving to each other in this early "honeymoon phase" of the relationship. At this point, our partner can do no wrong in our eyes. They are just so loving and open, strong and beautiful, stable and reliable. We feel we have just "died and gone to heaven."

As the relationship continues, the complications of life intrude into our love nest, and things may become more stressful. Problems at work, money issues, health challenges, and family difficulties can arise. These outside factors always existed, but we may have pushed them aside to focus on our romance. Eventually, though, other concerns need our attention, and so these issues trickle into the relationship. It can be shocking to see our "perfect partner" become human, with "warts and all." The charming and charismatic object of our affection can now at times become worried, distracted, withdrawn, preoccupied, and emotionally unavailable. In some moments, they may feel like a stranger.

Suddenly, we don't feel as happy and our Inner Child doesn't feel so safe. The primary selves who have been somewhat "off-duty," since things were going so well, immediately come back in. They do this by engaging in their old patterns; as they do, it can feel like the honeymoon phase ends. Our primary selves reassert themselves and react in the ways they always have. And of course, our partner's primary selves also return and react in the ways they are most familiar with and prefer. After all, these behaviors have helped us get through life so far. When this happens, the very qualities that we so loved and admired in the other can become annoying and off-putting. Our lover's charming attention may begin to feel smothering and controlling, or they may feel distant and vacant. It depends on the primary selves' strategy and the shadow selves being revealed.

These changes can hurt so much at this point that many couples might begin doubting their relationship or consider leaving their partner. Since the relationship seems so different, they question whether they are with the wrong person. Typically, it is clear that the other is the one who's "wrong."

Many relationships might end at this point or follow an on-again/off-again pattern. The couple may also stay together but become entrenched in unfulfilling roles; often this is a painful battle of opposites, in which the couple flips between polarities.

The following story shows how this process can unfold in an ultimately successful way using the example of one couple, Lisa and Robert. Lisa is outgoing and social. She is an extrovert and loves being with people and having an active schedule. She likes to get together with friends often, and she values meaningful talks and deep connections. Relating with people is very important to her and takes up a large part of her time.

Robert is more of an introvert. He prefers to spend a good amount of time alone or with just one or two friends. His favorite pastimes are reading, spending time on his computer, or taking long walks. He loves being in nature, experiencing his surroundings. He feels connected with himself when he is outdoors in nature. He enjoys road trips and will travel for days, exploring on his own.

When Lisa and Robert met, they fell madly in love and adored these qualities in each other. Lisa loved that Robert initiated a lot of activities outdoors and that he valued spending time with just the two of them. She also admired that he took time for himself, since she found it helpful to have down time or quiet time for herself as well. His desire to have time to himself also gave her the opportunity to continue to be with her friends and pursue her usual range of different activities.

Robert found Lisa charming and engaging. Her interest in him and what he was doing made him feel special. He was relieved to have someone else initiating social engagements and planning dinners with friends. He appreciated being with someone with an active life; this gave him plenty of time to himself, and he did not feel he had to be responsible for his partner.

Lisa saw the value of taking contemplative time and wanted to have more of that in her life. She felt calmer and more grounded when she took time for herself. She saw that she already possessed these qualities, but she also recognized she needed more of them in her life.

For Robert, being with Lisa made him feel alive and active. Her efforts to connect with friends and family were something he wanted more of in his life. For both Lisa and Robert, they both recognized these qualities as aspects in each other that they admired and desired; they saw how these ways of being brought a new and better balance into their lives.

Their relationship worked very well...until they had their first disagreement. In the same way that we can admire our partner and learn about ourselves through our positive reflections in them, we can also learn about ourselves when we see negative reflections. When we have an argument with our partner, or when we are influenced by outside circumstances — such as when we are sick, tired, overworked, stressed, and worried — we see what is negative about the other and usually blame them for the "problem." We are instantly aware of what they are doing wrong!

When Lisa and Robert argued, Lisa said things like, "You *never* want to go out. You're *always* on your computer!" Robert would say things like, "You *always* want to go, go, go, and never slow down. You *always* have people around. We never have time alone!" These were painful experiences that made Lisa and Robert feel terrible. However, we can learn from these exchanges and find valuable information about ourselves.

This takes time and sometimes requires space. If each partner is able to pause, return the focus to his- or herself, and reflect on what they are feeling, they can begin to experience awareness. This process of awareness provides a lens into our inner process, guiding us toward caring for ourselves and leading us into healing. What was a painful experience in the relationship is transformed into a deeper connection and sense of intimacy.

These opportunities are not just in conflicts that arise. Whenever we find ourselves judging or criticizing our partner, we have an opportunity to learn about our process and ourselves. Of course, this is true for positive reflections as well, although these reflections tend to be subtler and allude to what we value and admire rather than what we are missing. The tensions and intense feelings that arise due to a conflict or disagreement spark an inner process like nothing else does. They often provide a clear path to exactly what we are lacking or suppressing within ourselves. As it turns out, this suppressed aspect is exactly what we most need to accept and embrace within ourselves to find the sense of ease, peace, and intimacy we are seeking.

Over time, as Lisa and Robert used their relationship as a teacher, Lisa learned how much she did in fact need to slow down. She needed more time to herself and more time to just "be." She saw that Robert was a teacher for her, showing her aspects within herself that would bring her an experience of greater balance.

Robert learned that he felt better when he was with people more often and had a more active schedule. He didn't want a schedule as busy as Lisa's, but she was a teacher for him, pointing to an aspect within himself that needed nurturing.

Lisa and Robert used their conflicts and differences to learn more about themselves as individuals, as well as how to grow closer to each other as a couple. This is the ideal. Bad moods, bad days, and hurt feelings are not always conducive to an experience of growing in consciousness. However, whenever we can approach a difficulty in our relationship with an open mind and as an opportunity to learn, both have an opportunity to experience greater intimacy and closeness. Some differences are obvious and can be quickly addressed, and some are more complex and can take many rounds of examination and levels of awareness before reaching resolution. Healthy doses of patience and tolerance are key.

However, not all relationships can or should be lasting. Sometimes, using our relationship as a mirror, we come to realize that, to care for ourselves best, we should leave the person we are with.

In the next chapter, Gina will share a story of one of her relationships that reflects this.

# Gina's Story:
# When Leaving a Relationship
# Is the Right Thing to Do

*This book isn't meant to be a "fix-it" book* or a "meet the partner of your dreams" book. It is truly about how we can use our relationships — all of our relationships, from superficial contacts to our deepest connections — as opportunities to become aware of who we are, all of who we are, and find healing and growth through that process.

Gina, my dear friend and collaborator, shared some of her personal experiences earlier in this book. She will now share another part of her story, a painful but important one.

Over the course of the many years in which Shakti and I have led relationship workshops, I experienced a life-changing event. It had its share of deep pain, but it resulted in the deepest inner work I've ever done. I knew that I could not help write a book on relationships and feel in integrity if I did not discuss what has happened in my own life. Shakti and I felt it was important to tell my story, and we both felt, strongly, the need to point out that not every relationship can be healed. In fact, sometimes the most healing act is to leave a relationship.

When Shakti and I first talked about working on this project together, I had no idea how the relationships in my own life would unfold and change. Shakti has often said, "The best way to do your personal work is to write a book. As soon as you begin to write, all your issues come up!" Since I had been teaching, leading workshops, and writing with Shakti for so long, I didn't think that necessarily applied to me. How long, after all, does one really need to do this work? Well, not only was my relationship with myself transformed, but my relationship with Shakti was transformed as well. My relationships with my children, my family, and my friends have been renewed, restored, and raised up. What a surprise this process has been: wonderful, joyous, and freeing at times, while very painful, discouraging, and confusing at times — and all of it was completely unexpected.

I have found that we are all in process with whatever we are working on at the moment. Each of us is growing and changing at our own pace, and in our own way, doing the best we can with the circumstances we are facing. Although we may have awareness about parts of ourselves, and parts of our lives, we can be completely in the dark when it comes to other areas of our lives or our relationships. We all have aspects that are unknown to us. We simply can't see what we can't see.

In addition to working with Shakti for many years, I have been in therapy on and off since I was eighteen. I got sober when I was eighteen and have maintained continuous sobriety and remained active in twelve-step programs since that time. I would describe myself as a seeker, and I devote much of my time to discovering my relationship with God (as I understand it), growing in my understanding and faith, and relying upon a power greater than myself.

I have been on silent retreats, sat in *satsang* with gurus, been hugged by Amma, chanted with Buddhists, danced into higher consciousness, participated in rituals, reveled in worship, and held a daily practice of prayer and meditation for many years. I consider myself a confident, outgoing, self-empowered woman, and yet I still found myself in a painful, humbling, and abusive relationship.

The abuse culminated one night in my home when my husband assualted me while two of my children locked themselves in their room, terrified. This was the end of my eight-year marriage and almost the end of my life. Most painfully, it was the squelching of my spirit, a suffocating of everything that animated me and brought me to life. I had enough awareness in that moment to know that if I did not get out of my marriage then and there, I might not have another chance to leave.

To that point, like many people, my knowledge of domestic violence had been informed by television dramas, where the violence is obvious, and the case is ultimately wrapped up in under an hour with justice having been served. I had never identified myself as a victim of domestic violence, nor did I recognize myself in the fictional women on TV. I am a self-employed mother of three, an avid volunteer, active in my community. I am a soccer mom! None of this fits with my picture of a woman suffering from domestic violence.

About four years before the incident of violence mentioned above, I had attempted to get help — actually, in hindsight, I was attempting to get my husband to seek help. I didn't connect with any services for abused women, mainly because I didn't realize the amount of abuse I was experiencing. I just wanted my husband to get help and to stop being so angry. We had a daughter who had experienced a life-threatening illness, and I felt she deserved a "family," so my husband and I reconciled after a short period when I believed he was getting help.

Following my experience in 2009, a friend connected me with Center for Domestic Peace, a domestic violence advocacy and education organization in the town where I live. A generous, compassionate, patient, and supportive advocate helped me understand what was happening to me and how to take action to protect my children and myself. She was by my side for every appointment, every court hearing, encouraging me, holding my hand, and hugging me when I needed it.

Today, I am a survivor, a trained advocate, and a proud volunteer. I do not believe I would be alive, or my children safe, if not for all the people who work tirelessly to help victims of domestic violence. I am passionate about reaching out to any woman in my community, and now to any woman reading this book, who might be suffering from domestic violence. I think many of us have an image or stereotype of what a victim of domestic violence looks like. Indeed, before I got sober, I had an image of what I thought an alcoholic was, just as I later imagined what a woman who was being abused looked like, and in neither case did they look like me. I didn't see myself like that at all, and so I didn't seek help until it was almost too late.

Domestic violence is a crime that permeates all neighborhoods, socioeconomic classes, and levels of education. It affects everyone, business executives and stay-at-home moms alike. We all may have a unique story to tell, but with domestic violence and abuse, we also have a shared story of isolation, fear, and powerlessness. If you have a friend who is suffering, or a neighbor who is suffering, or if you are suffering, you are not alone. There is help for us all.

You can't change other people, and there is no way to change yourself so that your partner will not be abusive. Although this book shares ways for you to use your relationships as a path to becoming conscious, a relationship where there is abuse and violence is not safe, and safety must be the first priority. Be sure to protect yourself and your family first and foremost by removing yourself from danger, even though, like me, you may eventually use these techniques to find that the relationship has something to teach you about yourself. Domestic violence involves power and control and is a very dangerous pattern, one that escalates over time. It is important to recognize that in addition to physical violence, there are many other forms of abuse, including verbal, emotional, economic, mental, and sexual. Not all abuse involves physical violence, but all physical violence begins with one or more of these other forms of abuse.

Once I was able to leave the relationship and navigate the initial phases of the restraining orders, court hearings, and the process of divorcing, I began to explore the complex beliefs, behaviors, and selves that influenced me and the choices I made (or chose not to make) in my relationships. This was a humbling process, yet ultimately the key to my freedom — not just because I ended an abusive marriage, but because I broke out of patterns that had kept me locked into a certain way of being for a very long time. My marriage was the final stop in a long line of situations where I valued someone else's opinion over mine, compromised my values so that I might be "loved," and questioned myself rather than holding someone else accountable for their bad behavior.

I could see the seeds of these choices in my childhood home, particularly in the actions of my father. Though I was now an adult, my Inner Child remained terrified and wanted to be a good girl so others didn't get angry with me. I realized I was afraid of anger, even my own. This led to all sorts of problems. It is natural to get angry or express frustration, disappointment, or negative feelings. I didn't know how to express these feelings in a safe and healthy way, so I chose to stuff and ignore what I was feeling, harbor resentment, and feel powerless. I eventually chose a partner who was able to express anger, but unfortunately, he expressed it explosively, with threats and rage.

My marriage did not start off the way it ended. What it became happened gradually over time. It was a process, a pattern of anger and then apologies. Eventually, the apologies faded, the criticism increased, and I came to feel like I was walking on eggshells most of the time. I was attracted to my husband at first. He brought a stability I needed and a structured routine that was very helpful to me. These same behaviors, however, became controlling and restrictive over time.

My story highlights the familiar process where at first we are attracted to a person because they possess qualities we want more of in ourselves. Then we reject the person for the same qualities that originally attracted us. Keep in mind that we are talking about the essence of these qualities, energies, or selves, not the actual behavior being exhibited by the other person. As discussed in the previous chapter, often we are attracted to someone who exhibits energies that are the opposite of our own. This is often because we recognize that we need to learn to express those energies more freely.

For instance, the essential thing we need may be in the form of setting boundaries, being forthright, or being able to value ourselves instead of overvaluing others. We are always seeking wholeness, and people are attractive to us if they possess the qualities that might make us "whole." We have developed primary ways of being in the world and have disowned others; we still need all aspects, however, or at least access to them, if we are to experience the balance and wholeness we seek. That said, when someone expresses a quality in a negative way — when they become a "jerk" and act in a mean, hurtful, or unkind fashion — we aren't meant to emulate that. We don't also behave badly in order to integrate this opposite energy.

I hope that sharing my story has been helpful and that my reflections have added to your understanding of Shakti's work. I continue to learn from my relationships and grow in response to what I discover about myself. This work, combined with ongoing support and a rich spiritual life, has brought me deep healing and a joy I never thought possible. I am also unwavering in my commitment to helping others, as this, too, is a source of great fulfill-ment. My wish for you is that you find the freedom you are looking for in your own life and that you experience boundless joy and fulfillment.

NOTE TO READER: As mentioned above, there are many forms of abuse, including verbal, emotional, economic, mental, and sexual, in addition to physical violence. Not all abuse involves physical violence, but all physical violence begins with one or more of these forms. For information on domestic violence, seek-ing safety, finding support, and resources in your area, contact the National Domestic Violence Hotline at 800-799-SAFE (7233) or visit their website, www.thehotline.org.

# PART FOUR

# TOOLS *for* DEVELOPING
# YOUR RELATIONSHIPS

# Facilitation

*The process of facilitation* helps us learn about who our primary selves are and what some of our disowned selves might be. This is critical in the process of becoming conscious, so that we can see ourselves with a holistic view that recognizes the sum of all of our parts: "good" and "bad," what we like and don't like, what we share with our intimate friends and the parts of us we don't even want to acknowledge exist. Consciousness is simply awareness. With that awareness, we can find healing and growth.

The process of facilitation is best done with a trained facilitator. However, it is a simple technique and can be experienced quite easily with a friend as well as alone through writing. Later in this chapter, we will discuss the techniques of facilitation. Here our focus is on creating awareness. First, to give you a general idea of how facilitation works, we have included a transcript of a facilitation in which I interviewed Gina. This demonstrates how the process fosters awareness of the many different selves within us and emphasizes what it feels like to experience these selves.

To start, Gina and I sit across from each other. We begin with establishing that where Gina is sitting is in the "center position," which we hold as the position of awareness, a place where we can develop conscious choice through the ability to access different selves or energies.

I ask Gina to tell me a bit about herself and her life. Once she begins speaking, I can hear a theme being expressed, with a specific voice and energy, which is one of her primary selves. I ask her to move her chair to where she feels like the energy of that voice is. She moves to her right. I face her and begin to speak with what I recognize as her Responsible self.

SHAKTI: I just heard you listing out all of the things Gina does. So you're the part of Gina that does a lot and has a lot to do?

GINA'S RESPONSIBLE SELF: Oh, yes. Gina is very busy. I do a lot for Gina and her kids! I help her get them to school, make sure their homework gets done, and that they have whatever they need for school, sports, music lessons, etcetera. I also help her quite a bit at work.

SHAKTI: Yes, I appreciate that very much!

GINA'S RESPONSIBLE SELF: Yes, well, there is a lot to do at work, too. She has workshops and writing and lots to coordinate and manage.

SHAKTI: How do you help her with that?

GINA'S RESPONSIBLE SELF: Oh, I make lots of lists. I keep them around and add to them all day long. I cross things off when I'm done. I use lists to track everything that needs to get done and all the things she can't forget. She does a lot, and so I really am on task all day long.

SHAKTI: How long have you been in Gina's life?

GINA'S RESPONSIBLE SELF: Hmmm, let me think about that. I think I might have been there making sure the cells divided correctly! I've been there a very long time — all of her life.

SHAKTI: What was Gina's childhood like? Did she need to be so responsible when she was young?

GINA'S RESPONSIBLE SELF: Well, her home was pretty chaotic. Her father died right before her ninth birthday. She has three sisters and two brothers, and three of them were living at home when her father died. He was killed in an accident, so it was very tragic and unexpected. There was a lot to do, and she became her mother's helper. Her mother was very busy supporting the family, and she was overwhelmed with an illness as well. Gina had to help care for her younger brother, do homework with him, make grocery lists, cook dinner, and pack lunches, and so on.

SHAKTI: It was you who stepped up and did those things, wasn't it?

GINA'S RESPONSIBLE SELF: Yes, I did those things for her. I am the part of her that was responsible and got things done that she needed to do.

SHAKTI: Wow, you have had quite a job! Do you get tired or do you feel burned out?

GINA'S RESPONSIBLE SELF: I never thought about it. I guess, yes, I am getting a bit tired. She has been through a lot of transition in the last few years, so I have been helping her a lot in this time. I get overwhelmed when there is so much to do. But I can't really take a break either. That would be very lazy, and there really isn't time for that. It would be rather frivolous, actually, because there is still so much to do.

SHAKTI: I can see that. Well, you have done an amazing job in Gina's life. As her colleague, I really appreciate it, and I know that her kids benefit as well. So do the many people that she helps. Thank you for your help! I also hear that you can get overwhelmed, and when I talk to Gina, I will share that with her. Thank you for doing such an amazing job.

GINA'S RESPONSIBLE SELF: That is really nice to hear. Thank you. I feel really good just to talk. Thank you for listening.

SHAKTI: Okay, let's have you move back to the center position. [Gina moves her chair back to the center position.] Now, take a deep breath, and as you exhale, release the energy you were just holding. Try letting go of the thoughts you just had. Take another deep breath, and as you inhale, bring in the integrated energy of your awareness into your conscious self. Good...

Let's pause a moment before we continue. As you can see, the Responsible self is a strong aspect within Gina. Can you relate to what her "self" was describing? Can you identify your own version of this aspect within you?

This aspect is really active and carries what we call "doing" energy. Most of us have an aspect that is responsible, and it is common to have many primary selves that have a quality of "doing," especially in our Western culture. In addition to being responsible, we have selves that are driven, such as the Pusher. Our responsible selves can be closely aligned with selves that are caretaking, such as with the Pleaser. These selves are all about taking care of others and doing for others. When the Responsible and Caretaker selves are connected, then they are usually focused on being responsible for everyone around them and what everyone needs (or what we think they need).

Now we will continue with the rest of the facilitation with Gina, who has moved back into the center position of awareness:

SHAKTI: Well, she has a lot to say! And what an amazing job she does in your life.

GINA: Yes, she is quite amazing. She really does a lot, and she's constantly looking for what needs to be done, what others need, and fixing and doing things for others. I can see that she has been with me a long time and helps me with so much, but she can be exhausting, too!

SHAKTI: Now, that sounds like another voice. Why don't you see where this new energy feels like it is, and move your chair there. [Gina moves her chair to the left.] Hi, so you were just saying that another self in Gina is very busy, maybe even too much?

ANOTHER SELF IN GINA: Yes, she is so busy and has to do everything all the time. There is no time for anyone else, never time to read, no time to just hang out or do anything fun.

SHAKTI: So you are a playful self in Gina?

ANOTHER SELF IN GINA: No, I am not really playful. I am just into slowing down. Not taking on so many commitments, not doing so much.

SHAKTI: And this other self in Gina has her active all the time? Running from thing to thing constantly?

GINA'S BEING/RELAXING SELF: Yes, she has her going all the time, and making lists and getting her up early with everything that has to be done. On and on!

SHAKTI: What would you rather be doing?

GINA'S BEING/RELAXING SELF: Nothing, really. I really like to connect with people. I like to have a long time to be with a friend or go for a bike ride. I like running, too, but only if it is for fun. Not a training run or pushing. I really like to just be. I like reading, I like watching TV shows, especially the ones Gina watches with her kids. I love just being with her kids. No chores, nothing to do, just hanging out together.

SHAKTI: Yes, I can see you have a lovely energy, and I might like to hang out with you, too! In fact, I think I have on occasion!

GINA'S BEING/RELAXING SELF: Yes, we have. And that's where I would like Gina to spend a lot more time, slowing down, not hurrying. Enjoying the sun and the ocean — they're so healing!

SHAKTI: Does Gina spend much time with you? Or does Gina access you very often?

GINA'S BEING/RELAXING SELF: She has gotten much better about bringing me into her life. She makes more time for the activities I love and is working on having fewer commitments. She's even reading a murder mystery! Since she is always studying and learning, she rarely just reads a book for enjoyment.

SHAKTI: It has been lovely being with you. You are a powerful energy, and I am glad Gina has you in her life. She is very social and I am sure you play a part there as well.

GINA'S BEING/RELAXING SELF: Thank you.

SHAKTI: Okay, now move back to the center position. [Gina moves her chair to the center.] Now take a deep breath and exhale, releasing the energy you were just holding. Take another breath, and as you inhale, fill yourself with integrated energy. Now come back to your self that is now becoming conscious. When you are ready, open your eyes. How was that for you?

GINA: It's hard to shift back. I really like the way that self feels. The first self felt very familiar to me. This one does, too, but not in the same way. I feel like I wake up as the "Responsible self" and spend most of my day in that energy. I love the way the "Being/Relaxing self" feels, and I definitely know her. I just don't have her naturally in my life as much. I have to make it an intention to bring her in more often. When I connect with people, she is the energy that makes that connection possible.

SHAKTI: Now sitting in this center position where you are becoming conscious, can you have a sense of accessing both energies? Can you experience both energies at the same time? Have a sense of creating a space that's a container for both energies to be experienced and expressed. How does that feel?

GINA: Yes, that feels good. I feel like I can bring in the right amount of energy I need. So if I am with my kids, I can bring in more "being" energy. If I am at work, I can bring in more "doing" energy. I can have them together at the same time, and mediate what feels right for the situation. In that sense, I feel balanced.

Facilitation is a dynamic and compelling experience. Even if you do not discover a disowned self or shadow side, it is extremely helpful to experience the power of a primary self and how much influence that self has in your life. It can dramatically shift your perspective to experience the fullness of a primary self and then to shift out of that energy and see that self only as an aspect of who you are.

It is equally powerful to witness another person experience facilitation. In our workshops, we take time to facilitate each person and make sure that each person witnesses several sessions as well. At the end of the workshop, people often share that the part that had the most impact for them was to watch another person in their process and see how much they identified aspects within themselves through observing that experience.

Here are a couple more transcripts that give us good examples of common selves we share. This next one is a session we had with our longtime client Karl. Karl works full-time in the financial industry and has worked hard to provide for his family, including four children in various stages of college.

SHAKTI: Karl, you were just telling me a bit about yourself, your job, and your children. Sounds like you have a lovely family.

KARL: Yes, I am very proud of my children. I have worked very hard to give them a life I didn't have when I was growing up.

SHAKTI: Really? Tell me a bit about that.

KARL: Well, my father left when I was young. My mother worked at several part-time jobs to make ends meet. She loved us and did the best she could, but we struggled for many years.

SHAKTI: How did this shape your parenting?

KARL: I was determined to provide for my children no matter what; I would never abandon them.

SHAKTI: Okay, I can hear a strong self coming through. Why don't you move to the left or right of where you are seated, wherever that energy feels like it is most powerful. [Karl scoots his chair a bit to the right.] Hello! Karl was just telling me about his children and upbringing. He was describing some strong values he had about raising his children, and I thought that might be something you were involved with.

KARL'S RESPONSIBLE FATHER SELF: Yes, yes, I guess so. I am totally focused on taking care of my children and my wife.

SHAKTI: Tell me more about this or how you do this.

KARL'S RESPONSIBLE FATHER SELF: Well, I believe in working hard. I put myself through college. I have worked my way up. I would never let my family down. A father needs to provide for his children.

SHAKTI: So you're the part of Karl that is a hard worker and a good father. You are saying "I" when you refer to Karl, but we want to talk to you as the part of Karl that has these values and makes sure he does these things.

KARL'S RESPONSIBLE FATHER SELF: Oh, yes, that's right. I am the part of Karl that gets him to work hard and provide for his children.

SHAKTI: Are there other ways you make sure he does this job well?

KARL'S RESPONSIBLE FATHER SELF: Well, he has made a lot of sacrifices along the way, but I don't really see them as "sacrifices." It is what he has had to do for his family. He doesn't have anyone else to rely on, and he needs to make sure they are cared for and loved and provided for.

SHAKTI: Well, it sounds like you have been very successful in his life. He and his family have a lot to thank you for.

KARL'S RESPONSIBLE FATHER SELF: Yes, that's true.

SHAKTI: Okay. Is it all right if we go back to Karl?

KARL'S RESPONSIBLE FATHER SELF: Sure.

[Karl moves his chair to his left, returning to his original spot.]

SHAKTI: Okay, Karl, take a deep breath and see if you can have a sense of this self sitting next to you, but try to experience a little separation from it. See if you can see it as a part of you or a lens you can look at your life through.

KARL: Yes, I can see that. He is a force. He is very strong and reminds me of an ol' business tycoon.

SHAKTI: Yes, he is really a blend of two selves. One is what we call a Good Father, who provides for his family and others, and this can be emotionally, physically, or financially. Then there is also a Responsible self that is hard working and has a strong work ethic, but it, too, is about providing for the family. Now that you see this self as a part of you, what do you notice about its role in your life?

KARL: Well, I think I started out working out of fear and never wanting to go back to my childhood. But now I can see that I am a "Responsible Father." I take care of many people, in my family of course, but also friends as well. I make sure my staff and employees are getting what they need; I make sure we are generous with our bonuses and that we acknowledge people on their birthdays and anniversaries. I have a number of staff I have taken under my wing or mentored.

SHAKTI: If you are always thinking about others and how to provide for other's needs, how does that affect you and your needs?

[Long period of silence.]

SHAKTI: This is a good way to see this part of you as a self within you that is a primary self and very strong. Even as you try and separate and see it as a part of you, it comes through and reinforces its values and proudly asserts its accomplishments. There's nothing wrong with this, and this self has helped you quite a lot! However, the catch is that if you don't have some sense that this is only a part of you and not all of who you are, then you can get sort of stuck always thinking of others, or what they need, or how to help them. It does feel good to help others, and you are kind and generous for doing it. But to keep rejuvenated yourself or to keep the well full, you must be able to receive, and that's a different self. Separating from your primary self, even a little bit, allows you to receive from others, to find rejuvenation through rest or activities that fill you up.

KARL: Yes, I can see that. It actually feels a lot better to see it that way. As "good" as that self is, I can feel a sort of intensity or drive with it. The idea of allowing another energy in immediately gives me a sense of ease and calm.

At this point in a session, we would go on to facilitate the other side, or the energy that brings Karl "a sense of ease and calm." However, this provides a good example of a Good Father self and of someone with a strong primary self.

The next example illustrates someone's Inner Critic. We all have this voice inside of us. On a good day, the Inner Critic comes up with ideas that help us improve or create a better outcome in our situation. On a bad day, it feels like it is hitting us over the head, making us feel like we are our own worst enemy!

Here is a session with Sophia, an amazing artist. Her paintings are magical and inspiring, awesome and compelling. She experiences periods she describes as "feeling depressed," when she's unable to create anything for weeks.

FACILITATOR: Sophia, you were just telling me about some time recently when you were feeling discouraged. Want to tell me a bit more about that?

SOPHIA: Sure. Recently, I had a small gallery showing in a café. I was commissioned to create a new series inspired by the art at that showing. I was happy at first and excited, but after a few days I was totally uninspired and stressed about it.

FACILITATOR: Okay, can you move your seat to where you feel like that energy is?

[Long pause, then Sophia sits on the floor beside and behind her chair.]

SOPHIA: Okay, this feels like it.

FACILITATOR: On the floor?

SOPHIA: Yes, here on the floor. I just can't do more than this.

FACILITATOR: Okay, that's fine — it's totally fine to talk to me from there. Tell me about this project that Sophia has.

SOPHIA'S INNER CRITIC SELF: Yes, "Sophia" has... well, she had a show with her artwork, her paintings. She was asked to create a triptych, three paintings that go together but are painted separately.

FACILITATOR: That's wonderful! She said that she was excited about it!

SOPHIA'S INNER CRITIC SELF: Well, yeah, but then she didn't do anything about it.

FACILITATOR: Tell me about that.

SOPHIA'S INNER CRITIC SELF: Well, I had all weekend — I mean, "she" had all weekend to sketch it out and think about colors. She didn't do any of it! She just sat and wasted all her free time. Then she had to go to work on Monday and still hasn't started the project.

FACILITATOR: I see. Why do you think this happened?

SOPHIA'S INNER CRITIC SELF: Can I stand?

FACILITATOR: Yes, of course.

[Sophia stands and paces a bit.]

SOPHIA'S INNER CRITIC SELF: Well, she is very indecisive. She waits until the last minute and then scrambles to get it done. She starts with one color scheme and then halfway through changes it. It goes on and on.

FACILITATOR: I see. Is this something you can help her with?

SOPHIA'S INNER CRITIC SELF: She needs to just be disciplined about it. She needs to set the time aside and get to it. She worries about what she is doing and then procrastinates. She is a good painter, but she will never be successful if she can't follow through. One time, she had an open house for her artwork and had to cancel because she was "sick." It was really because she couldn't pull it together.

FACILITATOR: Wow, you sound like you feel strongly about this.

SOPHIA'S INNER CRITIC SELF: Maybe I do, but if I don't try and get her to see these things, she will never be successful!

FACILITATOR: So you are trying to help her?

SOPHIA'S INNER CRITIC SELF: Of course!

FACILITATOR: I see. Well, these are very important points you have made. In a minute I am going to go back and talk with Sophia. Is there anything you want me to make sure she knows from you?

SOPHIA'S INNER CRITIC SELF: Yes. I think she is an amazing artist. If she can work on this, if she's not so afraid and doubting all the time, she could really be successful. She has received a lot of recognition, but she needs to work on her method.

FACILITATOR: Okay, I see. Thank you for sharing. I will definitely convey your concerns. She is very capable, and I have a feeling she is going to be receptive to your ideas.

SOPHIA'S INNER CRITIC SELF: Thank you.

FACILITATOR: All right. Sophia, close your eyes and see if you can shift out of that energy a bit. It is quite strong and has some strong ideas. Take a few moments to allow yourself to relax and return to yourself.

[Sophia returns to her chair and sits down.]

SOPHIA: Ah, that's much better. Yes, that's a very opinionated self!

FACILITATOR: I can see why you might be feeling down or stifled.

SOPHIA: Yeah? How so?

FACILITATOR: She has some very strong ideas and is constantly on your case.

SOPHIA: That's true.

FACILITATOR: She means well, but the way she's on your case can feel like a bit much! She is actually very supportive of you and thinks you are a wonderful artist. She is worried about your process and wants you to be a success. If you can take the essence of what she is saying, it might be helpful.

SOPHIA: I can see that she worries and then stalls or gets distracted with other things to do.

FACILITATOR: Right. That voice we were just talking with is the Inner Critic. It can be very negative sounding and pessimistic, but it actually has our best interests at heart. It makes sure you follow the "inner rules" of your primary selves. You probably have a primary self that has ideas about being efficient or responsible. But the critic does it in such a way that it comes out like a put down, and it's natural for us to try to avoid criticism. It works off of negative reinforcement rather than positive.

SOPHIA: Yes, she's often putting me down.

FACILITATOR: Ultimately, your critic is trying to protect you from being criticized or judged by others. Or from its worst nightmare, being a failure! Most often in our work, when we ask a critic what it is afraid of, after a few rounds of, "Okay, and if that happens, then what?" it usually lands on something like, "I'm afraid she'll end up being a bag lady on the street." So, understanding how the critic operates, and how it actually has our best interests at heart, helps to neutralize the sting of what it says and how it says it. We can begin to partner with our critic and let it become a good guide for us. Sometimes I like to think of the critic as some kind of herding animal that's nipping at us to keep us in line for our best good.

SOPHIA: Yes, but I feel so discouraged and unmotivated.

FACILITATOR: Yes, that's how the other selves can feel when you have an overactive Inner Critic. Of course, you would feel bad about yourself and have an attitude of "why bother" if someone was telling you what's wrong with you all day! We certainly don't let our friends talk to us like that! Why would we let ourselves speak to us that way?

SOPHIA: Yes, how true! Well, I feel hopeful about this new way of looking at my Inner Critic. I can see how I often have trouble beginning a project because I am telling myself that I am not good enough or other artists are better or they use the right colors or have better technique, etcetera.

FACILITATOR: Your Inner Critic is telling you these things, but it's just a self within you, not "you." You, as a conscious being, can have the choice now about how much you let that voice influence you. You can bring in other energies to balance it, or you can take action on the guidance it is providing for you.

SOPHIA: Yes, that feels more empowering. Thank you.

## FACILITATION SNAPSHOTS

Here are a few more samples from sessions, to give you some more ideas about how these selves interact.

Lucy has a strong Pleaser:

FACILITATOR: So, you are the part of Lucy that wants to make sure she is pleasing to others?

LUCY'S PLEASER SELF: Yes, I don't know if I would say it that way, but Lucy should be helpful and kind to others. She should be generous and giving. And happy, too! That's how we all should be. I mean, it's rude not to be. And I would never want Lucy to be rude. One time her boss wanted her to do something, and she thought she had a better idea, but I didn't want her to embarrass him, so I made sure she kept it to herself.

Martin has a strong Pusher:

FACILITATOR: You sound like the part of Martin that has helped him to become so successful.

MARTIN'S PUSHER SELF: Yes. I keep him moving forward. Never look back.

FACILITATOR: Is this just in his work life?

MARTIN'S PUSHER SELF: Oh no, I keep him moving, going, staying active in many ways. I have him knocking out projects at work, and he always has a project at home, too. I also have him in the gym six days a week. I always say, "Anything less than six days a week is weak." He signs up for at least two marathons a year and at least one obstacle course race. Oh, and at least two triathlons. Those are easy. Depending on the race schedule, he might opt for a half-marathon instead of a full, but that only happens when there are conflicting race dates.

Claire has a strong Perfectionist:

FACILITATOR: I see, so you are the part of Claire that makes sure she plans the party well and does a good job?

CLAIRE'S PERFECTIONIST SELF: Oh yes! Without me, the party would be a disaster, if it happened at all! I prepare the guest list eight weeks in advance. I make sure invitations go out at least six weeks ahead, and each invitation is color-coordinated with the theme of the party. I tuck in cute little reminders for each guest to put on their calendars or hang in their kitchens, office areas, etcetera. I plan the menu and check to see if anyone has food allergies. If so, I offer two options at dinner so we can accommodate any special needs. I plan the dessert to perfectly complement the meal, so that our guests enjoy a delightful meal, but they are not so full that they can't enjoy the entertainment at the party. I usually arrange for a musician, band, or karaoke, depending on the celebration. Oh, also at the party, each guest leaves with a photo of themselves with their date and a stamp on the back that coordinates with the invite from the event. It's so sweet to commemorate these parties!

## FACILITATION TECHNIQUES

For an optimal facilitation experience, we recommend working with a trained facilitator if possible. (Visit Hal and Sidra Stone's website to find Voice Dialogue facilitators: www.voicedialogue international.com.) We believe this is the best way to experience the selves. You can also work with a facilitator through live video chats or by phone. Facilitation is a simple process, though, and it can be just as powerful to do on your own or with a trusted friend.

Before working with a friend, we recommend that you and the person you will work with both read this book. You might want to consider talking about it first or discussing an agreement between the two of you so that each person's emotional safety is the priority.

You can easily do this process on your own as well. One way to do this is by writing questions with your dominant hand and then writing the responses with your nondominant hand, or vice versa. You can also use two different pages of a journal, or two different colors of pens, pencils, or crayons.

If you are a professional who would like to incorporate facilitation into your work, we recommend visiting Shakti's website (www .shaktigawain.com) or Hal and Sidra Stone's website (www.voice dialogueinternational.com), where you can find information on trainings, workshops, and additional materials.

The principle of facilitation is simple: by asking leading questions, we give an opening for the selves to talk about themselves. This is usually a very easy process; the selves are thrilled to have a chance to share their opinions, thoughts, and ideas!

If you are the one facilitating, whether working with a client or a friend, use the active listening technique — keep acknowledging that you are listening through nodding, verbal recognition, and eye contact. Once the person's self speaks, you want to repeat back to the self what you have heard and confirm what they are conveying. It is important for the self to feel heard. It is also important not to give your own opinions, offer advice, or take "sides." This keeps the process open for everyone in a way that feels safe.

Here are a few suggestions to help you get started when facilitating. You can name or identify what you sense the self to be and then ask:

> You're the part of [name] that gets angry about...
> You're the part of [name] that is excited about...
> You're the part of [name] that is worried about...

Or you can use inquiry:

> You sound angry. Are you mad?
> You sound worried. Is there something worrying
> you?
> You sound scared. Are you feeling frightened?
> You seem happy. Are you feeling excited about...?
> You seem relaxed. How are you feeling?

You can also address the general areas the self might be active in:

> You're the part of [name] that is involved in parent-
> ing...
> You're the part of [name] that is active at work...

Here are some good follow-up questions:

> How old are you?
> When do you first remember being in [name's] life?
> What was happening when you first were present?
> What were you like in [name's] childhood?
> What is important to you?
> What are the areas in [name's] life where you are
> most active?
> What role do you play in [name's] marriage?
> What role do you play at [name's] work?

These are meant as suggestions; they're just prompts to help you get started. Keep in mind that the goal is to give the self you are interviewing open space to talk about itself and its concerns. There often is very little for the facilitator to do in order to engage the self beyond creating the space for it to talk and then actively listening. Once we become aware that the ideas, judgments, or opinions we have are in fact from selves within us, there is a natural process that unfolds, leading us to awareness. This awareness brings about the change we have been aching for, ignites the growth we have been searching for, and inspires the passion in our lives and our relationships that we have been missing. This awareness is the beginning of our path to consciousness.

Facilitation is a powerful way to learn about our relationships with our selves and with others. I've also found many of the tools I've shared in my previous books to be extremely useful in this regard. I discuss two of them — Creative Visualization and the Core Belief Process — in the following chapter.

# Creative Visualization Techniques

Creative visualization is the technique of using your natural, creative imagination in a more conscious way to create what you truly want. Discovering the technique of creative visualization has been magical for millions of people around the world. It is being successfully used in the fields of health, wellness, spirituality, creative arts, psychotherapy, business, and sports, and it can have an impact in every area of your life.

When we refer to "visualization," it is important to mention that mental imagery is different for everyone. Some people may "see" images and pictures; others receive their information through color, sounds, and objects or experience a simple sensing or knowing. All these forms work, and however you experience it is just right. Just feeling your desired state of things is the most important thing.

One of the most valuable ways to use creative visualization is in improving our relationships. Although many people share stories of how they visualized their perfect partner and ultimately manifested this person in their lives (sometimes down to the smallest details), our focus in this chapter is on using the power of intention to improve our relationships on every level. We do this through imagining what it is we want to bring into the relationship. We may want to bring clarity and visualize clearing out old patterns of thought and behavior. If we want to improve the quality of our connections with each other, we might imagine strengthening our bonds and increasing a sense of intimacy and closeness. We can bring peace or a sense of harmony through practicing affirmations and meditations. We also can use specific exercises to open ourselves to what is trying to happen in our relationship or what the universe might be trying to bring to us.

When we are experiencing difficulty in a relationship, we can use creative visualization to bring about powerful change. This is most effective when combined with the other tools in this book. One way to do this is by simply recognizing the power of our thoughts. As we have seen, when we are in relationship, we are sensitive to the other person, and they are sensitive to us. We have an entire level of nonverbal communication with those closest to us. This sensitivity affects the thoughts, attitudes, and beliefs we have about each other. This is important because what we believe about a person or a situation shapes how we act or behave toward them.

Through acknowledging this naturally occurring process, we become empowered to change the thoughts, attitudes, or beliefs that are affecting us negatively. Through the power of our imagination, we can use creative visualization techniques to let go of old belief systems, to change our ideas about ourselves or another person, and to affirm new ways of interacting. In fact, our awareness of this process, in and of itself, can bring about radical change and healing. As we practice manifesting new ways of seeing ourselves, and those we are in relationship with, we can bring balance to our relationships. This begins a process of aligning our outward actions with our intentions. As a result, we bring consciousness to the entire relationship.

By using visualization, we are acknowledging that we have the power within us to make significant change. Through accepting this personal power, we can see how we play a role in creating and cocreating our reality. This means that if we accept that we play a part in creating our reality, we then have the power to change and influence what happens next. We accept and act on our ability to create positive change in our lives and within ourselves.

Taking this position compels us to look at how creating our own reality does not always result in a positive picture. Sometimes we don't like what we see when we evaluate our life or, more specifically, someone in it. If a situation or relationship is unacceptable, we can acknowledge that we have helped create this on a deep level, and therefore there is a purpose to what we are experiencing. The truth is that we get what we expect and ask for on the deepest levels. This is not about blame, pity, or being a victim, however. If we believe we play a part in creating it, then we believe we can play a part in healing it.

This is actually a way for us to become empowered and break old patterns. We can adopt an attitude of total responsibility. This is a powerful first step in using our relationships as a path of consciousness. As we pursue the idea that we have manifested the situation we find ourselves in, what we are trying to learn is revealed. In meditation, we can ask ourselves why we have created this situation in this way. Why have I manifested this person in my life? How is this person helping me to learn and grow?

If you have a genuine desire to experience a deeply fulfilling and happy relationship in your life, and if you are ready to accept this joy in your life, then you can and will create relationships that work for you.

## CREATIVE VISUALIZATION EXERCISES

Here are several Creative Visualization exercises to help with your relationships. For these exercises, we draw upon the most powerful techniques in Creative Visualization and the Creative Visualization Workbook. They can help you get to the point where it's natural to think creatively and to use your imagination positively. These are some of the simplest, most effective exercises we have used.

## EXERCISE
### *The Basic Creative Visualization Technique*

Here is the most basic creative visualization technique in four steps:

1. Pick a goal. Identify something that you desire to be, do, or have. For example: "I would like to be have better boundaries in my relationships." Or, "I would like to have a wonderful and fulfilling intimate relationship." Or, "I would like to have lasting love in my life."
2. Make an affirmation out of it. State it in a simple sentence, in the present tense, as if it were already true. For example: "I assert clear boundaries in my relationships." Or, "I

am now creating a wonderful and fulfilling relationship."
Or, "I am now creating lasting love in my life."

3. Picture your goal or feel it as if it were already true. Usually it's helpful to close your eyes and just pretend or imagine what things would be like if it were true. Don't worry if you can't picture the scenario clearly — just feel it or imagine it in whatever way is easiest for you.

4. Consciously turn your goal over to your higher self, or to the higher power of the universe, and let go of it. This means you don't try to *make* it happen; you relax and let the higher force go to work within you to create it. Then just go about your life — but be sure to follow your intuitive impulses and promptings, and be open to growing and changing.

## EXERCISE
### *Pink Bubble Technique*

The Pink Bubble Technique is one of the most popular exercises. We continue to receive regular correspondence from readers all over the world who have just discovered this exercise or are writing to share their amazing stories of using this powerful tool in their lives. This process combines the above four steps in a very simple, effective way.

Sit or lie down comfortably, close your eyes, and breathe deeply, slowly, and naturally. Gradually relax more and more deeply.

Imagine something that you would like to improve or manifest in a relationship, or perhaps imagine a new relationship that you would like to manifest. Imagine that it has already happened.

Picture it as clearly as possible in your mind, or simply feel or sense it.

Now, in your mind's eye, surround your fantasy with a pink bubble. Put your goal inside the bubble. Pink is the color associated with the heart, and if this color vibration surrounds whatever you visualize, it will bring to you only that which is in perfect affinity with your being.

Now let go of the bubble, and imagine it floating off into the universe, still containing your vision. This symbolizes that you are emotionally "letting go" of it, turning it over to the higher power of the universe to bring it to you.

You can do this process once and let go of it completely, or you can do it regularly for a while. If you want to do it regularly, I recommend doing it every morning when you wake up and again at night before going to sleep.

## EXERCISE
### *Writing Affirmations*

Take any affirmation you want to work with and write it ten or twenty times in succession on a piece of paper. Use your name, and also try writing it in the first, second, and third persons. Remember to use the present tense. For example:

> I, Shakti, am now creating a wonderful, fulfilling intimate relationship.
> Shakti, you are now creating a wonderful, fulfilling intimate relationship.

> Shakti has now created a wonderful, fulfilling intimate relationship.

Or:

> I, Gina, am now healing my relationship with my
>     mother.
> Gina, you are now healing your relationship with
>     your mother.
> Gina has now healed her relationship with her
>     mother.

Don't just write it by rote; really think about the meaning of the words as you write them. Notice whether you feel any resistance, doubts, or negative thoughts about what you are writing. Whenever you do (even slightly), turn the paper over, and on the back write out the negative thought, or the reason why the affirmation can't be true, can't work, or whatever.

For example, on the back you might write: "I'm really not good enough. I'm too old. This isn't going to work."

Then go back to writing the affirmation.

When you are finished, take a look at the back of the paper. If you have been honest, you will have a good look at the reasons why you are keeping yourself from having what you want in your life.

With this in mind, make up several affirmations you can use to help you counteract and clear these negative fears or beliefs, and write out these new affirmations. Or you may want to stick with your original affirmation if it seems effective, or modify it slightly to be more accurate.

Keep working with writing the affirmations once or twice a day for a few days. Once you feel that you've really looked at your negative programming, discontinue writing out your negative thoughts and keep writing just the affirmations.

## Exercise
### *Ideal Scene*

Writing out your "ideal scene" is another popular visualization exercise that we often include in our workshops. It is a powerful way not only to manifest in your life but also to affirm the deep work you are doing.

You can work with a specific goal you are trying to reach, for example, manifesting a fulfilling relationship, finding an ideal partner, or bringing healing to a relationship. Think of a goal that is important to you. It can be any long-range or short-range goal. Write down the goal as clearly as possible in one sentence. You might also use this exercise to help you find the right place to live or a job you are envisioning.

Underneath that, write "Ideal Scene," and proceed to describe the situation exactly as you would like it to be when your goal is fully realized. Describe your scene in the present tense, as if it already exists, in as much detail as you wish.

When you have finished, write at the bottom: "This or something better is now manifesting for me in totally satisfying and harmonious ways, for the highest good of all concerned."

Then add any other affirmations you wish, and sign your name.

Now sit quietly, relax, visualize your ideal scene at a meditative level of mind, and repeat your affirmations.

Keep your ideal scene in your notebook, on your desk, or near your bed, or hang it on your wall. Read it often, and make appropriate changes when necessary. Bring it to mind during your meditation periods.

One word of warning: If you put your ideal scene away in a drawer and forget about it, you are very likely to find one day that it has manifested anyhow — without your consciously putting any energy into it at all!

## PRACTICING THE BASIC TECHNIQUES

Now let's go through these techniques again so that you can work through them with a specific goal of your own.

First, pick a goal. It can be on an emotional level; for example, a warm, fulfilling relationship. It could also be something material or spiritual, such as a house, a visit to a loved one, or a job.

For this first one, choose something that is important to you, something that you can achieve and that is realistic but that demonstrates your goals and dreams. Take a sheet of paper and write your goal at the top in a simple, specific sentence: "My goal is…"

Next, state your goal as an affirmation by writing it as a sentence in the present tense, as if it were *already* true. Make sure you don't use words like "I *will* have" or "I *want* to do," as that places your goal in the *future*, not the present. Use phrases like "I *now* have,"

"I am *now* creating," "I am *now* doing," and so on. Keep your three versions of your affirmation as short and simple as possible.

Now close your eyes, take a few deep breaths, and relax your mind and body. Say your affirmation to yourself a few times and imagine that it is now true. "Try it on for size" and see how it feels to have your desire come true. Then imagine putting it into a pink bubble, tossing the bubble into the air, and letting it go.

Now consciously affirm: "I am turning this over to the higher intelligence of the universe within me, to guide me in creating it."

You can also repeat the cosmic affirmation: "This or something better is now manifesting for me in totally satisfying and harmonious ways, for the highest good of all concerned."

Now write an ideal scene for your particular goal. Write a few paragraphs describing this goal in as much detail as possible as if it were already true in the present. Write it in the present tense ("I am now...").

If you have any trouble doing this, see if you can mentally project yourself into the future, to the time when this goal has been fully realized. Then pretend you are writing a letter to your best friend, describing the situation in detail.

For example, if your goal is to find a new relationship, or if it is to improve a relationship already existing, write a description of your ideal relationship as if you already had it, describing what your partner is like, what you feel like, what you do together, what you do separately, your surroundings, and so on. Make sure to use positive statements. Don't place blame or describe what is "wrong" with a partner or another person or a situation. Simply state the ideal way the relationship or situation will be. This process also works for healing past hurts or experiences we are ready to let go of.

Don't underestimate the power of these exercises.

## EXERCISE
### *Forgiving and Releasing Others*

Here's another simple exercise to do that has powerful results — try it and see! For many of you, it might be the single simple key that opens you up to the intimacy you have been longing for.

At the top of a page, write: "The people in my life who have hurt me are…" Then write down the names of everyone in your life whom you feel has ever mistreated you, harmed you, or done you an injustice, or toward whom you feel or have felt resentment, hurt, or anger. Next to each person's name, write down what they did to you or what you resent them for.

Then close your eyes, relax, and visualize or imagine each person, one by one. Hold a little conversation with each one, and express the anger and hurt that you have felt. Tell them exactly what they have done to upset you and what you want from them. Once you have done this, explain to them that now you are going to do your best to forgive them for everything and to dissolve and release all constricted energy between you. Give them a blessing and say: "I forgive you and release you. Go your own way and be happy."

When you have finished this process, write across the paper: "I now forgive you and release you all."

When you finish this exercise, you can tear this page out and throw it away, as a symbol of letting go, or just write "FORGIVEN AND RELEASED" in big letters across the page.

### EXERCISE
### *Forgiving and Releasing Yourself*

In this exercise, you focus on forgiving and releasing yourself. At the top of a new page, write: "The people in my life whom I have hurt are…" Then write down the name of everyone you can think of in your life whom you feel you have hurt or done an injustice to, and write down what you did to them.

Again, close your eyes, relax, and imagine each person in turn. Tell them what you did, and ask them to forgive you and give you their blessing. Then picture them doing so.

When you have finished the process, write at the bottom of your paper (or across the whole thing): "I forgive myself and absolve myself of all guilt, here and now, and forever!"

When you finish this exercise, you can tear this page out and throw it away, as a symbol of letting go, or just write "FORGIVEN AND RELEASED" in big letters across the page.

Forgiving and releasing others and yourself clears away internal emotional blocks to intimacy. Old hurts may hinder our ability to be open and vulnerable with our current partner. Regrets about how we have behaved in the past can make us feel unworthy of love. This exercise is useful in all aspects of life, but you may also focus specifically on forgiving old relationship hurts you have felt or inflicted.

You will see and feel the effects of these exercises immediately. They show us the way on our path to conscious and happy relationships.

## EXERCISE
### Core Belief Process

This process has proven to be very effective for many people. It is best done with a partner, but you can also do it alone. If working with a partner, one of you asks the questions and the other answers them. Take about two or three minutes for each step. Then switch and have the other person ask the questions, while the second person answers.

If you do this process alone, you can write down your answers to each question, answer them silently to yourself, or speak into an audio recorder and listen back.

Sit silently for a moment, eyes closed, and get in touch with that part of yourself that is powerful and responsible — perhaps the primary self who you see as the creator of your current experience or the self who can most help in this situation. Be sure to work to integrate the opposite self, too, into this exercise so that the selves work together. Now think of a particular situation, problem, or area of your life where you need to expand your awareness or become more conscious, such as a boss you don't get along with or an ex-husband who shares custody of your children.

Now complete the following steps:

1. Describe the problem, situation, or area of your life that you want to work on. Take a few minutes to talk about it generally.

2. What emotions are you feeling? Describe the emotion — such as fear, sadness, anger, frustration, guilt. Do not describe the thoughts you are having about the situation, only the emotions you're feeling related to it.

3. What physical sensations are you feeling?

4. What negative thoughts, fears, or worries are you having? What "tapes" or programs are running in your head? Take three or four minutes to describe these thoughts.

5. What is the worst thing that could happen in this situation? What is your greatest fear? Suppose that happened. Then what would be the worst thing that could happen? What if that happened? Then what would be the *very worst thing* that could happen?

6. What's the best thing that could happen? Describe the ideal way you'd like the situation to be — your ideal scene for this area of your life.

7. What fear or negative belief is keeping you from creating what you want in this situation? Once you have explored this question, write your negative belief in one sentence, as precisely as you can. If you have more than one, write each of them down.

8. Create a clearing affirmation to counteract and correct the negative belief. Here are some guidelines:

   a. The affirmation should be short, as simple as possible, and meaningful for you.

   b. It should be in the *present* tense, as if it's already happening.

   c. It should use your name. For example: "I, Shakti, am a worthy person. I deserve to be loved!"

   d. The affirmation should *directly* relate to your core negative belief and turn it into a positive, expansive one.

e. Your affirmation should feel exactly right for you. If it does, it will likely cause a strong emotional feeling. If it's not right, try changing it until it is.

Some examples:

NEGATIVE BELIEF: "The world is a dangerous place. I have to struggle to survive."

AFFIRMATION: "I, Gina, now live in a safe, wonderful world. The more I relax and enjoy myself, the safer I am."

NEGATIVE BELIEF: "I don't deserve to be loved," or "Relationships are such a struggle."

AFFIRMATION: "I, Shakti, have wonderful relationships in my life; I deserve to be loved!"

9. Use your affirmation in the following ways:

   a. Say your affirmation silently to yourself in meditation, picturing everything working out perfectly.

   b. If you have a partner, have your partner repeat your affirmation aloud to you, using your name and looking deeply into your eyes. After they say it, you say, "Yes, I know!" Repeat this process ten or twelve times. Then you say your affirmation and your partner says, "Yes, it's true!"

   c. Write your affirmation ten or twenty times a day. If negative thoughts arise, write them on the back of the paper, then keep writing the affirmation on the front until you feel clear about it.

# Conclusion

*You may find yourself asking,* "What's the point of all of this?" Or, "Why should I do all this work?" Or maybe, "Why dig up past memories and painful feelings? What's done is done." Our answer: *freedom.* Freedom from patterns that have held us back, kept us in relationships that weren't right for us, or kept us bound by our past. Having freedom means we have renewed permission to choose how we behave, how we make decisions, and who we are intimate with. This freedom comes as a direct result of doing this work. It is the product of digging deep and looking honestly at ourselves, taking our everyday experiences and turning them into opportunities to see ourselves in a whole new light. This freedom is made possible by our ability to access the different aspects within ourselves and move forward from a conscious place.

Through our newfound freedom, we are able to share this liberation with those we are in relationship with, especially our families and those we are intimate with. Once we embrace all of who we are, we find a new level of acceptance and tolerance for others as well. We are able to extend them forgiveness in the same way we have been able to forgive ourselves. As we learn to see ourselves in a new light, we see others in a new light as well.

As we find healing for ourselves, we find healing for our families, including our families of origin. We shift the weight of responsibility we have placed on those who raised us and find some ease or peace with our past. It is not that we now think that everything in our past was fine, or that what happened doesn't matter, it is just that we don't need to repeat the wounding experiences over and over or stay stuck in our past waiting for something to change. By doing this, we release others from being stuck in the past, too.

We realize that time has passed and we are here now. Today we are empowered to move beyond our past and find new ways of being in our lives and with our family. We get to let the others in our lives be who they are, as we now give ourselves permission to be who we are. We give them the dignity to have their stories and selves and ways of coping, just as we have. The key to this freedom begins with an attitude of openness as we discover awareness, explore acceptance, and find conscious choice.

We view our relationships as *paths* because they lead us in the direction of healing and growth. They offer us an opportunity to use the reflections we see in others as insight into our own process, especially understanding where we might need to take our process next. By holding this perspective, we are able to approach interactions in an entirely new way. We can use our reactions, even our negative feelings and experiences, as events that can bring us our greatest healing and growth. With this new outlook, the possibilities are endless.

As I set out to write this book, Gina and I had many ideas we wanted to convey, experiences to share, and tools to pass along. A main goal was to offer the Relationship Workshop in a book format. Our hope was to make this material available to readers who could not travel to see me or attend a workshop.

During the writing of this book, I decided to retire from leading workshops. This made my goal with Gina even more pressing. I also wanted to offer a book that was less a "how-to" book and more of a "How can I use this difficult opportunity in my life to grow?" book. We intentionally chose the title "Handbook" because we wanted this material to be helpful and referred back to time and time again like a reference. Gina and I hope you have found this material useful and helpful in the way we envisioned.

As Gina and I were finishing up, we realized this is not an ending but a beginning. The beginning of our next adventure! This is true for all our paths: when we arrive at an ending, we come to realize it is in fact a beginning. We hope this will be the start of something special for you — possibly a whole new way of being in your life and in your relationships. We wish you the best on your journey of discovery!

# Acknowledgments

*We would like to thank* the team at New World Library, especially Marc Allen for his personal support and contribution to this project. Also a heartfelt thank you to Georgia Hughes, our editor, and to Kim Corbin, our publicist, for their grace under pressure and never-ending patience!

We would like to thank Judy Vucci not only for being Gina's mother, but for her willingness to read every version of the manuscript we handed her and for her significant contribution to our workshops and this project.

Shakti would like to offer special thanks to her husband, Jim Burns, for his love and support and for traveling this path with her. Special thanks to her mother, Beth Gawain, for her pioneering spirit and for remaining her biggest fan.

Gina would like to offer special thanks to her family and friends, especially her children, for their support during the many evenings and weekends she worked on this project and missed spending more time with them. (I love you dearly, Sawyer Dedmon, Cole Dedmon, and Anabella Long!) A special thanks and shout out to her group Girls with Swords, Jeff Mazzariello, Luz Alvarado, and Malia McKinney for their kindness, love, and wisdom.

Finally, we would like to express gratitude to all of you who have attended our workshops over the years. We are inspired by each of you and by your unwavering commitment to your healing and growth.

# The Voice Dialogue Work of
# Hal and Sidra Stone

*Hal Stone, PhD, and Sidra Stone, PhD*, met in Southern California in the early 1970s. Hal was a Jungian analyst and Sidra was a psychotherapist. They were colleagues for many years and shared a deep friendship. They eventually married and became life-long partners. Today they live and work in Mendocino, California.

When they began their relationship, they were very much in love. Their relationship was very affectionate and fulfilling. They had both been married previously, and both had children from those marriages. Over time, they began to realize that similar patterns from their previous relationships were being repeated. Issues arose from their blended families as well. Finding themselves in this difficult place, they committed to working through the challenges they were experiencing. They were determined to stay together and to keep their relationship alive and romantic.

They began to delve into their process, examining their patterns, and gleaning insight into the dynamics of their relationship. As they continued, they realized that they had similar behaviors in their less-intimate relationships as well. Through this revealing experience, they developed a process that helped them tremendously to shift these patterns.

First, they realized that they each experienced different, and often conflicting, ideas or perspectives within themselves toward a given issue or situation. They explored these different aspects and discovered that behind these seemingly conflicting perspectives were actually "selves" or voices who were expressing them. It was as if they had many subpersonalities that worked together to make up their complete personality. These selves had their own opinions, thoughts, and reactions. Hal and Sidra began to facilitate each other by talking with these different selves. Through this process evolved the technique of Voice Dialogue and the body of work that they called the Psychology of Selves and the Aware Ego.

Eventually, as they shared and taught this work, they reached and trained people all over the world. They continue to grow in their understanding of this work, and they are constantly evolving and expanding it, integrating what they learn along the way. Discovering this work was the key for them to find freedom in their relationship; it created a framework for resolving any of the issues that have arisen in their thirty-year journey together.

Their work is a comprehensive body of psycho-spiritual work, relating to and drawing from many other disciplines, including Jungian analysis, Gestalt therapy, and psychosynthesis, to name a few. Their work is so broad and all-encompassing, however, that it goes many steps beyond anything else we have ever found. It has been extraordinarily helpful, both in our own personal healing process and in our work with others.

Much of our understanding about the many selves within us, and the importance of developing the Aware Ego, comes from studying and working with Hal and Sidra Stone. The depth of their understanding of selves is quite profound, and the method they have created for getting to know and understand our many subpersonalities is one of the most powerful tools for consciousness that we have ever experienced.

Hal and Sidra are wise and wonderful authors and teachers who continue to lead workshops and trainings as well as publish books, CDs, and DVDs. Their websites are www.voicedialogue international.com and www.voicedialogue.org.

# About Shakti Gawain

Shakti Gawain is a pioneer in the field of personal development. For over twenty-five years, she has been a bestselling author and internationally renowned teacher of consciousness. Shakti has facilitated thousands of individuals in developing greater awareness, balance, and wholeness in their lives.

Shakti has written numerous books considered classics in her field. Her distinguished publishing history includes the bestsellers *Creative Visualization, Living in the Light, The Path of Transformation, The Four Levels of Healing, Creating True Prosperity,* and *Developing Intuition.* Her books have sold over ten million copies and have been translated into more than thirty languages. She is the cofounder, with Marc Allen, of New World Library.

She has appeared on such nationally syndicated programs as *The Oprah Winfrey Show, Good Morning America, Sonya Live, Larry King Live, Leeza, America's Talking,* and *New Dimensions Radio,* and she has been featured in *New Woman, New Age Journal,* and *Time* magazine.

Shakti is a passionate environmentalist who believes that as we bring more awareness to our daily lives, we can learn to live in balance on our planet. She and her husband, Jim Burns, live in Mill Valley, California. Her website is www.shaktigawain.com.

# About Gina Vucci

*Gina Vucci* has worked with Shakti Gawain for over fifteen years. Having been personally mentored and trained by Shakti, Gina coleads workshops with Shakti, facilitates groups, and has contributed to Shakti's bestselling products. She is a fierce advocate for women, children, social justice, and the environment. Gina has worked in several fields as counselor, mentor, and coach for individuals and small businesses. She brings a deep level of experience, wisdom, and joy to her work with others. The mother of three inspired children, Gina lives in Northern California. You can read her blog at www.soccermomspirituality.com.